MOURNII

by

Sue Lamb Brown

An Autobiographical

Journey of Faith

A Farmer's Daughter

Goes from Grief and Crisis

to the

Light of Jesus'

Hope and Healing

Mourning Song © 2019 Sue Brown

Scripture taken from the King James Version unless otherwise noted.

Cover design by Stephenie J. Stubblefield

This book is dedicated to Iris.

Iris and I met at a church we both attended. Shortly after we became friends, she was diagnosed with a cancerous brain tumor. Iris was a warrior with a gentle spirit and was an excellent example of grace under pressure. Above all, she was a woman of Faith. She didn't win her battle with cancer; she graduated to Glory after a valiant and courageous battle. Oh, but the testimony she lived that inspired so many! I want to have that kind of impact on people.

Many other courageous friends have fought and lost their battles; some are still fighting. They have all fought the good fight, with courage, honor, determination and strength: and above all, Faith.

Faith is the substance of things hoped for, the evidence of things not seen. Hebrews 11:1

One day all who have lost loved ones in Christ Jesus will be reunited at a glorious reunion in Heaven.

What a beautiful day that will be-- Eternity with the Lord and our loved ones!

It is my hope and prayer that as you read this compelling story, you will be blessed, encouraged, and infused with Hope in the Lord.

Acknowledgements:

How do I even begin? So many people, so many events have occurred in bringing this book to fruition. This journey would not have been possible without the circle of family and friends the Lord has blessed me with.

First and foremost, I praise the Lord for His watch care over me and my family. Without Him, we would be nothing, and would not have a story to tell. I am grateful for every friend who stood by us in our troubled times and picked us up, helped soothe our tears and set us back on our path toward healing and wholeness.

My family is blessed with a loving and encouraging, supportive church family. We love each of you and are so thankful for your continued love and care for us. Our pastor, Dr. Will Stone, has been a caring and compassionate encourager, counselor and friend to us all. He is dedicated in his resolve to preach the Word of God.

There are many people who were significant encouragers and cheered me on along this writing journey. My family has been the most awesome, supportive tribe of any I know. I am "bursting at the seams" proud of each one of them. It is a large tribe, so naming them would be another book. They know, they understand, and will continue to be my most avid fans. My heart is filled to overflowing with their love and care. They have a lot to watch out for, especially in dealing with "little 'ol me."

I am so thankful for friends that have encouraged me and given me resolve to get the words in print. Pam, Robin, Al, Rachel, Mike, Hugh and so many others were my strongest cheerleaders. If I have neglected to mention you, please forgive my oversight and know how much of a blessing you were to me in this endeavor. I could not have done it without your love and support.

I'm thankful for my patient husband, Stephen, who endured the quiet house and the "shushes" when I was writing, deep in thought and didn't hear what he was saying. I was quite distracted at times.

I so very much appreciate the heritage that my parents gave me. My parents' concern and care for all of their kids through the years has been a compelling motivator to keep going in the face of adversity. They faced adversity, met it head on and overcame.

I am ever grateful to my friend Suzanne, who fixed all my silly grammatical and sentence structure mistakes that I was befuddled over, and then, had the audacity to actually enjoy doing it! I will be very careful not to use the squiggle ~~in writing. ~~

I am thankful for enduring friendships. My good friend Sheila, who encouraged me, challenged me and answered tons of questions. She was gracious enough to offer her knowledge, experience and assistance in the publication arena to bring this book to completion. I am ever grateful for her.

Last, but not least, I am thankful for an artist in the family. My daughter Stephenie dug deep, set her emotions aside, and did the amazing watercolor painting for my cover. It is perfect.

All of you are and will continue to be an inspiration to me.

Contents

He alone is our refuge and strength, our very present help in time of trouble (Psalm 46:1).

Chapter One: How It All Began...

His mama had gotten up with him and helped fill the wagon with produce from their meager garden. As he trudged down the hot and dusty dirt road, his feet were blistering from relentless heat; his pants were too short, threadbare, worn out at the knees. He needed a break, a respite from toil and dogged determination that was driving him, compelling him to keep going. He was thirsty, discouraged, and tired. Spying an old, weathered, majestic oak, the lad pulled his wagon under the cool, swaying branches, retrieved his lunch from the belly of the wagon and sat beside the trunk of the tree. Up early before the sun rose, he was exhausted, weary from picking his produce. He peddled squash, peppers, tomatoes, rutabaga, collards, and turnip greens, anything that would grow in the sandy soil of Florida.

Being abandoned by his father, saddled with responsibility as the oldest son for the large family so recently deserted, he squared his shoulders and returned to the task at hand. By the time he made his rounds in the largely poor neighborhood, he had some change in his pocket, and his wagon was emptied of its produce. He returned home, satisfied he did his best.

This lad was my dad, who continued to be a caring and responsible individual as he navigated his youth, dealt with a broken family, attended school, worked various jobs, and dealt with all the conundrums that life threw at him. He later married a beautiful, feisty local gal, and began the adventure and challenges of having a wife, starting a family, and buying his first piece of land he could call his own. That dogged determination—that he was blessed or cursed with; however you choose to look through the prism of his life—eventually helped my parents to be successful with a farming operation in Cottage Hill, Florida.

My mother and father at his prom.

Chapter Two: Crushed, Broken in Spirit

Part of our farming operation was raising purebred registered Duroc and Tamworth hogs. We frequently showed them in the local county fairs and state fairs, winning many blue ribbons for the quality livestock and showmanship that we kids learned in the 4-H club. Dad usually began small and built up an operation as he had time and resources. We had a farrowing house, a finishing barn for the feeder pigs, and another barn with stalls for the sows and their piglets— a maternity ward, if you will. Yet another area was fenced off and kept the large boars that serviced the corralled females. Frequently, we had to move some of the livestock to different areas and rotate them.

One morning Mama, my little sister Mary (who was the baby and about three and a half years old at the time), and I were in the small field where the feeder pigs had been housed to graze and root about. I'm sure some of my brothers were helping, but I have no recollection of who else was there. My job was holding a gate shut or opening the gate as requested. It was not a small gate, but a twelve-foot farm gate that was hung somewhat askew. Mary was watching all the activities from a distance and stood behind the gate. When Mama told us we could go to the house, and being the kid that I was, about seven or eight years old, I just let go of the gate and started to run back to the house. Unfortunately, Mary was standing in the path of the fast swinging gate; it hit her and knocked her flat on her back. Of course, she started crying at the top of her lungs. I stopped in my tracks and turned to go back to her, and as I did, Mama started yelling at me in her stress, anger, and frustration. I left, weeping, crushed, broken, wounded.

Mama had NEVER spoken to me that way before; I didn't know what to do. As I retreated to the house, I was confused, not understanding her outburst at me. I was a child, and she had expected me to think rationally about laws of dynamics, cause and effects, that I was not quite capable of considering at the age I was. Nothing was ever said after that about her tirade. I suffered silently and tried my best to stay in her good graces to avoid the pain and sting her words had inflicted on my tender heart.

This incident began a new mindset for my life—one of working diligently to please others, to avoid their displeasure toward me or anything I did. I became determined in these efforts and learned many skills that would help all of us about the farm. My personality was developing, and I was drawn toward keeping the house, including the cooking, sewing, and domestic activities. I enjoyed the outdoors, the farm, and all the activities with its hustle and bustle of everyday living but inside was where I felt most appreciated. Being able to help in the house boosted my damaged self-esteem and helped me feel valued. It also took some stress off Mama as she directed the boys and assisted them with the assigned chore list of the day.

My father, still involved in farming at an advanced age

My mother

Chapter Three: A Grandma's Love

Shortly afterwards, Mama began giving me basic lessons in cooking, and I would start supper, cooking round steak, gravy, Spanish rice, or anything she asked. When I forgot, or didn't understand or know what to do, I called my grandmother, (who lived down the road from us) and asked her how to do something or the technique in cooking a food item. Later, as an adult, I remembered these phone calls and realized how inconvenient and untimely they must have been. It must have been such an interruption to what she was doing on her own farm. Grandma never chastised me, nor was critical of these calls. She epitomized a true grandma's heart in her love and care of all her grandchildren. I wanted to be just like her!

My grandmother was a wonderful grandmother. She had fourteen grandkids, all living within a mile of her farm. It was a short trek through the woods to get to her house. We could go the long way, which was down a graded dirt road, past the neighbor's growly dogs, when we felt we could peddle our bikes fast enough to outrun them. Sometimes we would take a chance and go the roadway; they could hear us coming and would leap out from the shrubbery and chase us. It gave us such a heart fright!

Grandma, as we all called her, was a soft-spoken individual. She loved the Lord and was diligent to help her grandchildren attend church and know about the Lord. I would get ready for church and watch through the living room window for her car to come down the road. I would then go to church with her. It was because of a faithful grandmother that I came to be saved, to have relationship with the Lord, to become a daughter of God.

My grandmother

Her last professional photograph

She was an outdoorsy woman and loved flowers and working in the yard. When we would sneak off the farm and come for a visit, our greetings would be a hearty "yoo-hoo!" We would listen for her return "yoo-hoo" and head in the direction of her voice. Sure enough, she would be on her knees weeding a flower bed. She always took time to visit, to listen to our angst, our complaints about anything we were going through. She was a good listener, yet she always gave wise counsel if it was needed. All of her grandchildren lived close by and enjoyed the benefits of her loving care.

Ann, a cousin who loved our Grandma dearly, was visiting one day at the same time as I. We were in the Mimosa tree, climbing and picking the soft, fuzzy pink blossoms. I said something to her about "my grandma" and she lit into me with an emphatic "she is not your Grandma!" retort. Well, I knew she was and proceeded to set her straight! Neither of us was wrong, but because of our young ages didn't realize the relationship and connection or the family dynamics. Grandma soon set us straight with a gentle explanation of our family and then offered us cookies and milk. All was righted in our little girl world, and we continued our play and grew up to be good friends. Our family lost Ann to cancer; it was a very sad day for me, to lose her. I believe she was the first cousin I lost. I will always remember that she and I had a special bond, a connection with each other that was unique.

Chapter Four: Middle Child, Oldest Daughter

There are seven of us kids in the family. I am the exact middle child, with three boys above me on the rung of the family ladder, and two girls and another brother below me. What is unique about my position in the family is I am also the oldest daughter. I am also the oldest granddaughter, the first girl-child on both my maternal and paternal side. This position presented me with some freedoms as well as challenges for my enjoyment. I'm sure Mama was elated to have a little girl after 3 boys; my parents have never told me, and I really haven't asked about their thoughts. It never occurred to me to ask, and now I can't ask my Mama, as she passed away in 2008.

Since there were three boisterous boys ahead of me, and Mama had a big workload on the farm and about the house, I learned at an early age that I could not be entertained by her. I remember playing on a quilt, outside under the pine trees, while Mama, Daddy, and the older boys repaired and built fence. She always packed cold water in mason jars, with cups to drink from. She put it in the shade to keep it cool longer. The jars would sweat because of the humidity.

I never developed what I refer to as "middle child syndrome." While I was probably neglected in some way because of our ever-expanding family, the attention I was lacking did not cause me to be a needy person. Nor did I ever feel there was any emotional weakness because of it. I did suffer from the usual growing pains during adolescence, and there were sibling issues to deal with, as most kids experience who grow up in large family. Big brothers are protective; they are also teasers and can have impish mean streaks in them. Mine certainly did!

As I grew older, I was assigned chores to help ease Mama's workload. I really believe it was to give me lessons in responsibility and work ethic more than anything. And as the other kids came along, my chore list would change, and the younger ones would take over the lesser chores. As I developed more skills, Mama entrusted me with more responsibilities. One of them was some general cooking. When she had to be outside on the farm, she would give instructions on what meat to get out of the freezer, and how to prepare it. My favorite meat to cook was country pork ribs. They were easy to do! Thaw them out, season them on both sides, and put under the broiler! We had a wall mounted oven with broiler pan underneath at waist height; it was just right for me!

I was also learning baking skills and was known throughout the community for making skillet pound cakes. Whenever there was a covered dish at church, that's what I would fix. There was nothing but an empty cake plate to bring home! I made the boys a lot of boiled oatmeal cookies as well.

Our neighbor up the hill didn't have any children, so she enjoyed the neighborhood kids dropping in on her. She usually had a treat ready; one of our favorites was Potato candy, made from boiling an Irish potato and mixing that with confectioner's sugar, rolling it out and spreading peanut butter on it, then re-rolling it and chilling it for a bit. It was served by slicing and putting out on a candy dish! I enjoyed visiting with Mrs. Lorraine; she was a kind and generous person.

Chapter Five: Crime, Punishment...Rewards!

Tractors were necessary, even required for a farming operation, especially when a farm does row cropping. All of us kids learned to drive one, as well as the heavy-duty trucks and stick shift vehicles. My first tractor driving was done on a Farm All tricycle. We had 153 acres to drive around on, and we took every opportunity to have a turn! That same tractor was the one I was driving when I had my first accident!

One of our cousins was spending the night at the farm. We had extra energy for some reason and wanted to drive the tractor around the neighborhood. There was a lovely full moon, visibility was great, and of course, I was eager to show off my driving skills. The other girls were getting ready to come to the tractor shed, so I ran ahead and cranked it up. It spit and sputtered to life. I hadn't anticipated it being hooked to a trailer, and I had to back it out, and that's one thing I had never done. In my zeal to impress, instead of asking one of the brothers for help, I tried to back it out. Unfortunately, I turned the steering wheel the wrong direction, and ran over the tongue of the trailer. I was rescued, but my Dad was not pleased. Everything that got broken cost him time and money, and both of those were in short supply those days. I was meted out punishment: I had to pick five gallons of wild blackberries. I got lucky that week!

It was blackberry season, and Mama knew where there was a hedge of large ones, succulent and juicy, on the south property line behind our pond. Saturday morning Mama and I got our buckets and water to drink and took off. It was quite a distance from the house; there were cows in the pasture that we had to look out for. One of those cows was an ornery, mean bovine. She was a Texas longhorn with shorter, curved up horns. Texas Longhorns are not very stout, they are rather lean. This one could and would run you over if she had a mind to! It didn't help matters that we kids would taunt her; no wonder she was mean and troublesome.

We managed to get to the back fence where the berries were without incident. I have no recollection if I picked the five gallons of berries or not. I just remember my fingers were stained, and I was hot, sweaty, and got tired of picking berries.

After this experience, I became more diligent to not make mistakes, to not bring anything on my head, so to speak, that would cause me trouble! Our family had a fair share of tension, pressures of life, and circumstances that caused friction. Dad worked full time shift work at the local paper mill, often taking extra shifts. He was also farming 153 acres, row cropping, plus had cattle and swine operations. Mama was also working hard helping on the farm and managing a large brood of rambunctious kids. Teamwork is essential in making an endeavor like theirs work. They were trying to build a successful hog operation with registered livestock suitable for showing in the local and state fairs. My parents became 4-H leaders with a club that met monthly at our home. The oldest boys trained steers for the local FFA (Future Farmers of America) chapter at school, and as the saying goes, the rest is history. We all joined in and learned how to show steers and pigs in the ring. Many of our

12

livestock won blue ribbons, and some went on to be exhibited at the state fair. Later, they were sold at auction.

As I remember, we all had to grow "thick skin" to weather some of the tension and pressures of our busy farm life. I also became aware that I needed to stay out of the way and accomplished that by immersing myself in the household chores. I loved to hang clothes on the line and enjoyed cooking and learning new recipes. It was a good way to defer the outside chores to my younger sister, who detested being inside. We often traded chores; I would double up and do her assigned household tasks, and she would do the ones I had been assigned for outside. That system worked very well for us for most of our growing up years.

These were formative years, years of horseplay, practical jokes, and brothers teasing and aggravating sisters, the usual sibling angst and rivalry. We didn't have a lot of spare time on our hands, and we didn't get to have much of a social life. But what we did get was determination, resolve, and a work ethic that was hard won. We understood working together to accomplish goals.

I was developing social skills from interactions with people in the church, when we had time to go, as well as when I was out and about on errands for my grandparents, my mama, or had to go to the farm store or pick up parts for my dad. Our farm chores were important, and usually precluded any outside activity. My observations of people and how they acted made many impressions on me, influencing how I would act or react to different environments.

After the planting season was done, we had a brief reprieve. Mama would pack a picnic supper, we would gather the floundering gigs, tubs and paraphernalia associated with that, and head to the beach for the evening. Such fun! We usually headed to the sound side picnic area. The best swings were there. I would pump and kick, getting as high as possible. Such a thrill it was, swinging high, with the moon coming up, the waves gently lapping at the shoreline. It was a short time of paradise at the beach. Those were glorious times, times of freedom to just be, no one rushing you, no one telling you to hurry up and get finished with a chore. We were kids, enjoying different scenery, different environment, a different set of parents; parents who relaxed and let us do the same. We all enjoyed our time of resting and relaxing; it was a welcome reprieve from the farm.

Chapter Six: New Life in Christ!

Somewhere about the age of eleven or twelve, I began to have a stirring in my heart that I was missing out on something important. I had gone forward at our Methodist church with my cousin, when she accepted Jesus as her personal Lord and Savior. I didn't make a profession of faith at that time. I was going with her, at her request, because she wouldn't go up front alone. It was shortly after that we were memorizing scripture verses to earn a spot to youth camp, all expenses paid.

Scriptures began making sense to me, and I began to read and understand more than just the typical sweet Bible stories I had been taught. It was becoming personal, with heart and soul-stirring meaning for me. Not long after, there was an altar call again, and the same cousin and I went forward together. The Holy Spirit made His impression on my heart, and I knew I was a sinner, that I wanted to ask Jesus into my life and heart. This time, she went with me! I was sincere and earnest in my desire to accept Jesus as Lord and Savior. Many parishioners gave me hugs and wished me well. I didn't know it at the time, but the enemy of my soul would attack me and try to get me to turn my back on the Lord. As I left for home, I could sense a change in my heart and mind. It would be a challenge to live my new found faith out at school, home, and in the community. I would be tested.

Testing comes with serving the Lord.

Scripture teaches us that truth: *beloved, think it not strange concerning the fiery trial which is to try you, as though some strange thing happened unto you: but rejoice, inasmuch as ye are partakers of Christ's sufferings; that when his glory shall be revealed, ye may be glad also with exceeding joy (I Peter 4:12, 13).*

There was a thriving youth group at our church. It had several adolescent kids my age attending, as well as older teenagers that were doing some leading. I could participate in the group, gain new friends, and help in outreach ministry. Those were good things to do, some I enjoyed doing more than others. I was developing a desire to help, to please people, to see something that needed doing, and either volunteer or ask to assist. All the young people at that time were rural kids and had learned generally the same type work ethic I had, so we swept floors after meeting, folded and put away chairs, and left our meeting room neat and orderly. Without saying it, our leaders were teaching by their example, and loving us in our sometimes unloveliness and moody temperaments.

I was so busy growing up and being active with school, church events, and home life, I didn't recognize that I was fast becoming a young adult. I began babysitting for extra spending money. I was also involved in 4-H, raising chickens, and selling eggs for a modest profit. In these ventures, I learned fairness in my business dealings, responsibility for caring for livestock, as well as being a person of my word, including showing up on time and taking good care of the children in my charge. I was developing character traits that would serve me well as I came into adulthood.

About this time, a new family moved into the neighborhood. They were retiring Navy people, with three boys in tow. Needless to say, all the girls in the neighborhood stood tall and took notice! We were silly teenagers and weren't really interested in the boys that we grew up with. But these new boys were good lookin'! Lo and behold, they came walking in the doors of the Methodist church one Sunday morning. And of course, I was shy, stood at a distance, and observed. That evening, the new boys attended the Methodist Youth Fellowship (MYF) and meeting. Introductions were made; we settled in and enjoyed the activities. They registered for high school, and classes began.

The youngest of the boys had the nicest blue eyes, the middle one played the piano impressively, the oldest was serious, reflective, and had chocolate brown eyes. I especially wanted to get to know the oldest one! He was slightly taller than me, was a knowledgeable student of the Bible, and had a gentle yet commanding presence about him. Of course, I attended MYF every chance I got! We soon became friends. We would pass each other in the hallway at school and say hello. It made my heart pitter-patter just to see him. I began losing weight, coming home from MYF meetings and going straight to bed, forgetting I hadn't eaten supper. I had a bad case of whatever it was! My dad even noticed, saying to me one afternoon, "Best be careful and eat. You'll dry up and blow away in a big wind."

As time passed, the young man started to notice me. He noticed that I was a helper and would pitch in to do whatever needed doing around the church. My attention to children was noticed, and as they gravitated to me and enjoyed being with me, he was considering I would be a good mother. He was aware of my growing relationship with the Lord as well. Oh, you bet, I was noticing some of the same attributes in him! He was knowledgeable in the word of God, got along well with his peers, was respectful to adults, and responded in a loving manner toward his brothers and parents. Well, ok then! I filed it all back to dream about later.

About this time, (I was sixteen years old) Dad was working shift work at St. Regis, the local paper mill, farming full-time, and had signed on to be farm manager for the state veterinarian. Mr. Vet had a farm in central Alabama, and he needed someone to manage his operation. Dad traveled to and from his farm on his weekends off, and would work long, hard days on the farm position, then travel three and a half hours home, shower, grab a bite to eat, and do his shift at the mill. He did this for a few years. It became evident he just wanted to farm full time. He scouted for land to purchase, finally found some and talked to the seller. He made a deal, made plans and arrangements to close down the farm where we lived, and relocate to God's country: Alabama. Our new farm was three miles from any "small" country store, there wasn't a big town less than twenty-five or thirty miles away, and it was in the middle of absolute nowhere! What do country folk DO for entertainment? Our family would soon experience the adventures and disappointments this move to a "foreign country" would give us. It was so rural that the area was frequented by a rolling store!

After he retired from St. Regis Paper Mill, my parents sold the original farm, moved lock, stock and barrel, animals, kids, and goods (there probably was a raccoon or squirrel or some pet varmint as well) and started over.

This new adventure, full of known and unknown possibilities, was ripe with fertile soil for row crops, good pasture for raising livestock, creeks for the kids to explore, woods full of nature and hunting potential, and a wonderful place to finish the task of raising a large family. The location was in a vast expanse of largely agricultural area. And thus, began an intriguing journey in the dead of winter, specifically January 1971.

Chapter Seven: To Go...Or Stay Behind?

Just a few short weeks prior to our departure for the unknown, my parents offered the possibility that I could finish out my senior year and live with my grandmother. That was a generous, totally unexpected surprise. I was a senior at the local high school and should have graduated that June. You see, the brown-eyed guy and I were high school sweethearts by then. I was crazy in puppy love, star studded, silly love with him. However, he wasn't so sure. He had plans, goals to achieve after high school, and a girl was not in his spiritual vision at the time for what the Lord was calling him to be, a medical missionary doctor. I had a decision to make, and a short time frame to make it in. Did I stay and enjoy all that my senior year offers? Or, did I go and share in the newness of a different high school, keeping family intact, and embracing all the changes along with them? I was torn, perplexed with my decision.

As I contemplated my dilemma, I realized the unfairness of the offer. I wanted to stay behind, to enjoy my last year of high school, and didn't want to leave this young man and the potential relationship that could very well blossom into a beautiful, enduring, and committed marriage.

After all, ever since I could remember, my life goal was to be a wife and mother, to care for children and home, to be a nurturer, have a husband that loved and cherished me, treated me with gentleness and respect, and would be an attentive, caring, compassionate, interactive daddy.

I sought an answer through prayer and godly counsel, knowing I had a desire to help my siblings with the changes that would impact them as well. They had to leave their home, their schools, their friends, and didn't have a choice in the matter, as I was given. We were re-assured by my parents that we could return for regular visits just like we were making to go to the new farm. This helped to tip the scales for me; I had made my decision. After I told my parents what I had decided, I sat at my desk, got out pretty stationery, and penned the answer to Stephen. I felt such a sense of relief, a burden lifted, a ton of weight off my shoulders. I was going with my family, and it would have to be okay. This is where the Lord was prompting, guiding my heart and mind.

We managed to write each other weekly. I returned to his high school graduation; he came to mine. Our love blossomed; we continued growing in love with each other, challenging each other in our relationship with the Lord, and tried to get a visit in every six weeks or so, as time, finances, and schedules permitted.

Chapter Eight: Adjustments, Reality

My family moved into a building that was not yet ready for habitation. Dad had purchased a barracks building from Ft. Rucker, Alabama, hired movers who cut it into three sections and relocated it to our farm. Two of the sections were joined together in a "T" formation for our new home and the other salvaged and used for building materials. Dad was working diligently to get it winterized, but it took time and resources to get settled. Essentially, we camped out for the first winter. Our saving grace was learning new skills and applying ones we knew. We quickly adapted and managed to get through the rough patches. We survived a bitterly cold and damp winter, a cold that went to our bones and made our teeth chatter. It was also a wetter than usual winter. When we left for school (we had to drive as there wasn't a bus route where we were), we wore our old farm shoes and toted our good ones in a bag. The Alabama clay stuck like glue to our shoes and caked on. When we were finally in the car, we switched shoes so we could be presentable.

Just a mere 200 miles north of our old homestead we had left, the cold and humidity were very different. We were accustomed to Florida's milder climate. Our paternal grandmother made a large quilt for us. She pieced together whatever fabrics she had available. The batting or filling was burlap: heavy, coarse burlap. The "quilt" was so heavy we couldn't turn over or change position once we were under its confines. I guess she thought we were going to the wild country of Alaska or something! That thing did its job, and somewhere along the way it was given away, or used for a barn drape for one of the baby calves.

There were adventures, mishaps, joys and disappointments for a while. After I graduated from the local high school, I worked in a commercial coat factory near where we lived. I then transitioned to a fabric store after I began having issues with the chemical odors in the factory.

Chapter Nine: College Life

I applied for college at Troy State University, along with financial aid, was accepted and another new adventure began. I had never gone out of town on a long trip much less left home before. I was scared, exhilarated, and nervous. Adrenalin carried me through much of this time, getting moved in, and acclimated to dorm life. It was a sad day for Mama when she unloaded the car, helped tote my stuff upstairs, and hugged me bye. Our apron strings were cut; I would never go home to live again, just to visit. Or so I thought. I met many wonderful young women (and a few guys as well) participated with the Baptist Student Union, and discovered I was homesick! All the changes, new friends, navigating college schedules, and finding classes, were a challenge to me. Somehow, fortified with determination and true grit, I did that (and a tad more) for five quarters. I was not a good college student. My new found freedom, a lack of diligent study habits, as well as social activities with my friends, brought my grades down and my college goals to a screeching halt.

I no longer had a lofty goal of being the world's best teacher; I was basically passing time until "love and marriage" could and would find me. It was an expensive life lesson; a work–study program enabled me to be there as long as I was. Although I would depart for future unknowns, I was grateful to have had that short time away at college. I grew up while there and learned much about life. When working for your money, learning how to budget and do without some necessities to stretch my living allowance was a necessity.

Meanwhile, the boyfriend and I maintained a long-distance courtship. He came to visit me at college, and we would go back to the farm for the weekend. Those were fun days, taking walks along the railroad tracks that crossed through the property, washing copious amounts of dishes together, as well as an occasional date to a Mexican eatery. He drove a red, four-door, stick shift Datsun. Returning to the campus, we took the back-country roads. It was fun to drive these roads with him, sometimes singing, usually just enjoying each other's company. Saco Road was a favorite; that car zipped around the "s" curves and hugged the road well!

After five quarters of schooling, the money that supported my educational endeavors was almost depleted, and I was forced into taking time off to return home and work for a season, with plans to return in the fall. Even though I did not walk away with a Bachelor of Science in Education, I did walk from the campus with good friendships, a renewed sense of self-confidence, as well as hope for good tomorrows and unlimited possibilities with what I could and would do in my life.

Disappointment settled in as I headed back home. I found a job at a fabric store as well as a rhythm and routine to my daily, mundane life. I helped on the farm when I wasn't working, doing whatever was needed. Most of the time, help was demonstrated by cooking large quantities of food for the family. Those three brothers and whatever farm help was around were hungry! Appetites were not easily satisfied when they were in the hayfield, baling hay, tossing the bales, stacking and unloading into the barn, and doing it over and over for days. Fortification for the hard labor involved food and copious amounts of it. Hydration was paramount for them as well. I loved taking gallons of tea and water, along with a snack of some sort, and glasses packed in boxes, a basket or metal bucket. We found the nearest shade tree, parked the truck, and called everyone in for a well-deserved break. Relaxing in the shade, most often with a slight breeze, we could let our thoughts wander, and enjoy the outdoors and each other's company. One of the boys would flake out on the ground with a cap over their face and catch some shut-eye. Someone would play a practical joke on an unsuspecting resting soul. There was always energy for horseplay!

Respite ended, we gathered empty glasses, packed up the leftovers, and headed home. We had to think about the next meal, and what we would cook. Work had to be completed in the field, before the rain set in, so gauging the time for supper was tricky at best. It was often hit or miss, and the food would get cold and need to be re-heated. Weary, dusty and tired, muscles aching from repetitive work, the men folk came dragging in, ready for showers and a hot meal. We kids often had to take dad's boots off. That was not a task for the faint hearted. After a day of sweating, grimy work on the tractor or combine or hay baler, his feet smelled to high heaven and desperately needed to be aired out!

I digress from intentions of my story. It is odd how one trail of explanation leads back to a childhood memory, yet these recollections are a part and parcel of who and what I am as an individual.

What we do, how we live, what we are exposed to in our childhood very often shapes and defines who and what we become in adulthood.

I am so grateful for all of my childhood journeys. Each one helped to mold me into a productive, independent, and fully functioning adult, contributing to society and my community.

Chapter Ten: Love and Marriage, and a Baby Carriage

Long about September of 1973, Stephen and I were discussing our long-range goals for the future. He was in his third year of college, struggling with calculus. His employment was at the local plywood plant. His hands were calloused and rough from handling the sheets of plywood repetitively. He was working the night shift, which made it easier for him to attend classes. The struggle with calculus was causing him to reconsider the medical profession. He would not be able to proceed without that class. He also began feeling unrest about his desires to be a medical missionary doctor, as admirable as that was.

In October of that year, I came "home" to visit. We were sitting on the couch at my grandmother's house. He quietly asked me to marry him! This girl was elated! Of course, I said yes! We sealed the deal with a kiss, and then he presented me with a small but gorgeous diamond ring. I wear it to this day, with love and honor.

The one caution I was given toward my desire to marry Stephen came from my mama. His intentions were to get through school and head to the mission field. In a foreign country of course!

Mama wisely spoke to me with genuine love and concern. Her caution was that I would be leaving all that I knew and loved and for me to consider seriously the emotional cost of such a decision. Her words of concern rang very true to my heart. I did weigh all those considerations. With prayerful reflection, my mind was made up: I knew I wanted to marry him and be his helpmate as God intended.

We planned a small December wedding. A cousin and my two sisters stood beside me as bridesmaids. Stephen chose three of his closest friends to act as groomsmen. We asked my Uncle Lewis to officiate; he was a man of faith whom we both loved and respected. Our reception was simple. Wedding cake, dinner mints, nuts, and Danish wedding cookies, along with punch, comprised the light refreshments for our guests.

After greeting everyone and taking some pictures, we left in his little Datsun car. Our destination was a cottage on the bay, a lovely secluded place. It was a wedding gift to us for the weekend and wasn't too far from home, as we had to return to school and work the following Monday. The honeymoon chase was on! His brother and a friend let us go for a time, waiting in a parking lot at the foot of the bridge they knew we would travel for our honeymoon. We tried to lose them, but after a while they gave in, and let us find the cottage without their escort or annoyance.

We were relieved at finally being left alone and looked for the correct address of our cottage. Driving after dark, in an unfamiliar location, we saw blue lights bleep behind us. Hubs pulled over. The trooper asked for his driver's license and then proof of marriage license to verify our story. Mr. Trooper smirked, wished us well, and let us proceed. We were now newlyweds and honeymooners. We walked the shoreline, the docks, discovered and enjoyed married life. I cooked for my husband, and we had dinner out some. We also attended church that first Sunday of married life, setting a precedent for our home.

Reluctantly returning to real life, we unpacked our stuff and set up house. One of the days of our first week together, we visited with Grandma, and also to pick up some wedding gifts. Cousin Ann was there. She very proudly informed us we had gotten married on the longest night of the year! It was the Winter Solstice! Well, I'll be! Talk about being embarrassed at that grand announcement! We had considered all the events and dates, and thought we had chosen wisely, to avoid conflicts with family celebrations and Christmas programs and festivities. In retrospect, we chose wisely. We settled into a routine of going to work and Hubs attending college and keeping up with course work in the evenings. He was still struggling in calculus, and this was a critical turning point in our lives. He began to feel drawn to another career choice but wasn't settled about what.

In our second year of marriage we had joyful news to share. We were expecting our first baby! Excitement isn't an adequate description of our feelings. Nervousness, anticipation, wonder, awe, and somewhat alarmed concerns aptly spoke to our newfound happiness. Questions came along with contented settledness in our hearts and home. Would we be good parents, could we "afford" a family, and how would we provide for this soon coming bundle of joy?

The Lord began to impress on Hubs that change was coming, but it would require trust and dependence on the Lord, a step of faith on our part. I had to trust that my husband had our best interests at heart, and that he had indeed heard from the Lord about this new direction. Getting closer to our delivery date, Hubs had a chat with his dad. After much prayer and counsel, it was confirmed that he would apprentice for one year under the wise direction and training of his dad, who had an established business in the piano tuning and repair field. Dad was hoping one of his sons would be able to take over his clientele when he chose to retire, and this was the beginning of that process.

What timing! He turned in his resignation from the dairy supply company where he was a delivery truck driver when our baby was three days old. Our first little girl was named Christy. I had pre-eclampsia during the last month of my pregnancy and was bed-ridden at home. I spent my days waiting by reading. One of the books I read was *Christy* by Catherine Marshall. I loved the spirit of her main character, and so we named our girl after her.

We were young, naïve, and had rose colored glasses on. To view our world through the lenses of a sense of joy and wonder was and has been an extreme blessing to our family. Routines of caring for the new baby fell into place. Hubs became adept at changing diapers and walking a fussy baby. He couldn't feed her, as she was nursing, but he did an excellent job of caring for our daughter.

We lived a quiet and simplified life, by choice and necessity. Money was tight, so in the evenings we enjoyed our time chatting and playing with the baby, who was changing and developing into toddlerhood before we were ready! Stephen was developing his skills on the guitar, writing songs, and singing the popular Christian choruses of the time.

On a particularly rough day, home from work, tired, discouraged, concerned about expenses, he was strumming on the guitar, with the now toddler's toy bag off to the side of the room. It was a gift from her grandmother, who was a seamstress and made a "Winnie the Pooh" themed toy bag. All the characters of the story were in the fabric design. Thoughts and words came into being, and before we knew it, a new song was born, "The Animal Song." Its message was essentially don't be discouraged, "don't hang down your ears like a donkey, but follow your Lord like a lamb."

That song became a cherished and favorite one out of his song journal. It is one our grandchildren request whenever he has his guitar out. A song of encouragement, remembrance of where we were and how far we have come.

Chapter Eleven: Understanding Adulthood - Pressures of Life

Our family was growing! Baby number two was soon to arrive, and there was no room in our current small mobile home. It was time to shake up our familiar routine and consider what to do— whether to stay where we were renting or look for another property to settle down for good.

Scripture teaches us that *"the steps of a good man are ordered by the Lord, and he delighteth in his way" (Psalms 37:23).*

This verse has deep meaning for our family, as you will see in "the rest of the story," as Paul Harvey used to say. That being the case, we followed His direction, as a door opened up for our provision. We accepted a gift of land from a beloved family member.

The necessary steps were taken to install electricity, plumbing, all the things required to set up our new home. Uncle Frank and Stephen hand dug the very large rectangular hole needed for our septic system as well as all the field lines. They laid gravel, measured for level, laid the pipes and completed the project, *by hand*, with lots of sweat equity investment. We shopped around and located a nice, solid and clean, larger and also newer mobile home to establish our residence. It took a few weeks to do all this, and in the meantime, the new baby was getting ready to make her appearance! We sold our current home, stored our few earthly possessions in the in-law's garage, and moved in with them until our home was ready— about three weeks. And of course, the due date for baby was quickly approaching. Panic mode set in, as we worked feverishly to get moved. Electricity was the hold up. The local energy company wasn't in any big hurry to get power installed, so this frantic, expectant mama called and used the "new baby coming better get to crackin' plea" and it worked. We quickly got power, and we moved in.

We had taken Lamaze classes and were prepared for a home delivery attended by a midwife. The baby came in the wee hours of the morning; we barely had time to call the midwife and finish a few last-minute preparations before baby girl made her entrance. The midwife still hadn't arrived, and I was in active labor, so Daddy stepped in and delivered her, cleaned her up and wrapped her. He tenderly handed her to me, and she nuzzled into my chest for nourishment. About an hour later, the midwife finally arrived. Her car had broken down halfway to our house. (She lived about twenty-five miles away). After checking mama and baby out, filling out the birth certificate, and visiting a bit, she gave instructions and went back home. We named her Stephenie, after her daddy who delivered her.

In a short fifteen months, baby girl number three arrived. Anna was also a home birth. Much to our relief, the midwife arrived in plenty of time for this delivery. Our first midwife had retired by this time, and our family physician referred us to a new midwife. We welcomed each baby into our hearts and lives, loving and caring for them as gifts from the Lord.

We had a reprieve from babies for three years, and husband *really* wanted a son. I was skeptical that we would get a boy baby, so I asked him for a guarantee, knowing the probabilities were just 50/50. Our next child was a son...a son. God had heard his request and granted it. He was delivered at the hospital as there wasn't a licensed midwife available at the time. We named our first son Robert. Of course, with three girls and one boy Hubs was outnumbered and wanted another son. After all, boys needed more boys to play with. Bless the Lord, He heard the Hubs request. Just twenty-two months later, baby boy was born at home with a midwife and weighed nine pounds, ten ounces! And hence, Andrew joined our family. I was done! Our family was complete after number five.

Our young family

Chapter Twelve: Parenting a Large Family

Parenting a large family is not for cowards or the faint of heart. We had many challenges, many joys, and some disappointments along the way. What we lacked in financial resources was more than made up in abundance of love to go around. We had a desire to raise good, well-balanced, and productive children into adults that would contribute to the greater good of family, neighbors, friends, and society. We accomplished all these things and more, by the grace and mercy of God, His right hand of righteousness, much prayer and support from our extended family as well as our church family.

Our story is written one moment, one word, one line, and one paragraph….one chapter at a time. It is written on the litmus paper of life, tested and proven over and over again with many joys, momentous occasions, and happy moments. And then, there are the unexpected events that alter our lives forever, leaving us with shredded heart and soul, a broken and empty vessel, an innate drive to prove the power of a loving and living God; a Creator who loves, with much compassion, an abundance of grace and mercy, to bring forth emotional and spiritual healing with a desire to perfect anyone who will trust and be willing to be broken.

Our experiences, whether good or bad, how we respond and react to them, speak to our families, neighbors, acquaintances, and friends as to whom we are, what we are made of, what we believe. Our choices, our knee-jerk reactions to the events that happen in our lives, steer our lives for the better, or worse and will have what is sometimes called a domino effect on everyone we are in contact with.

We continued on, going to work, building a business in the piano tuning world, getting the kiddos through school, unscathed and independent, ready for the real world of work and responsibility. Let's be perfectly honest right about now. We didn't do everything right; we made mistakes and had to apologize to our kids for wrongs of miscommunication and misunderstanding. One parent held the proverbial line, the other tended to be a softy. Two of our daughters sounded exactly alike in their voices. I would be in the kitchen, prepping for supper, overhear an argument, intervene, and had the wrong one in trouble. Other times, there were issues over lack of cooperation, an "attitude of ingratitude" among the growing pre-teens and teenagers in the house. Those were trying days, to say the least. We dealt with the usual teenage angst, sneakiness, some white lies, and pranks done in humor to siblings.

Through these difficult years, I frequently thought of my parents raising seven lively, rambunctious and adventurous kids. How did they manage a farm, Dad working full time at the local mill, and do all they did? They had to be exhausted, worn down from the workload of all they had taken on. They were leaders to a 4-H Club, Dad also raised purebred swine and showed them in the local and state fairs, we had show steers as well, and all of us were expected to participate and assist in these endeavors. I raised chickens and had them for my 4-H projects. We were a very active family with farm responsibilities and pressures to keep up.

In my wondering, I had a realization, that in spite of the filter of childhood memory, things were not always smooth, happy, and contented. There were pressures on both parents to keep things going, working the farm crops, and tending livestock, keeping the equipment operational, and the household going. "Many hands make light work" as the saying goes, and therein was part of the functionality of our life. We all had a part to do, workload to carry, and if anyone was slack it kept the rest from fully functioning at capacity. There were tensions between Mom and Dad, teenage angst would rear its rebellious head on occasion, there were tears, anxiety, and broken-down fences and people and machinery that needed mending, older parents that needed care and taken to the doctor or grocery store. We got home from school, looked at "the list" that Dad would leave and groan. It could be an extensive and exhaustive goal to get the things checked off in an afternoon and evening. Staying busy and working quickly to get the list clear was our goal; if we did, it was an accomplishment. That rarely happened, though, and some chores had to carry over to the next day. It was the only way to keep up with expectations.

Let's close the door on my childhood and take another direction. I share my past because it affected my future, what I was to become, and the character of who I was to be. I could share many fun and happy moments of our family, my marriage and home, events and misadventures that we had while raising our family. My focus is to expand and illuminate on God's plan for my life, His direction for our future and how *"all things work together for good to them that love God, to them who are the called according to His purpose" as Romans 8:28* states. We have a greater purpose than living for ourselves, and this is the path I chose, am choosing, to set my feet on.

God has set the stage of our lives, getting things organized and ready for us, from the very beginning of Creation until we entered stage Left. He has written the script we will play out, as evidenced by Jeremiah 1:5:

"Before I formed thee in the belly, I knew thee; and before thou camest forth out of the womb I sanctified thee..."

He is a gracious God, and offers us free will to decide how we will live out our part on the world's stage, how we will enter, speak, feel, live, make decisions, and how those decisions will affect those to whom we interact with on a daily basis. Those decisions will impact someone's eternal destiny.

It is beyond my wildest imagination how God does this, holds the world together in His hands, and yet still has unlimited capacity to love and care for all of us. I am eternally grateful that He does!

Chapter Thirteen: Changes

As our children became young adults, leaving home for the adventures of college and military, I began having some medical issues. After consulting with my doctor, we chose surgery to "fix" the problem. I had a hysterectomy, and then shortly thereafter, I had a DVT, deep vein thrombosis, which resulted in a longer stay in the hospital and extended recuperation time. It was also a hindrance to HRT (hormone replacement therapy) which I needed but couldn't have. The hormones could have caused another blood clot. I had to "bite the bullet" so to speak and manage to control my imbalance of hormones without HRT.

That was one of the toughest years of my life. I wanted to escape to Australia, and my family wanted to escape *ME*. Our garden was the cleanest it had ever been that year, as the Hubs spent any free time hoeing it and beseeching God on his behalf for patience and fortitude to weather the storms I was experiencing. We can laugh at this now, but while going through, it was quite the opposite feeling. I was sad, angry at my fate and felt like a gray cloud was constantly weighing me down, hovering to suck what little enjoyment I had out of my soul. It was the worst of times, or so I thought. After a year of suffering, we were exhausted and needed relief. We eventually sought treatment for this medically induced chemical imbalance, and found a new balance that was manageable, that brought peace and calm. Yes, it was a prescription drug for depression, and I am so thankful for medicine that works. After a year of treatment, I sensed the Lord giving me peace and calm in my spirit, and slowly weaned off the medication. I have not needed it since.

This experience, even at its worst, would be used by the Lord at a later time, to comfort and help another family member who was going through a bout of depression. You see, I *understood* the gray cloud of depression, the feelings of hopelessness, lack of self-worth, of inadequacy! God does not waste our tears or heart's cry; he WILL bring good out of all the messes in our lives to **work together for good to them that love God, to them who are the called according to His purpose (Romans 8:28)**. (Here's that verse again!) God seems to be establishing a pattern here, in my life and my family's' lives, of proving this verse true to my family.

I can't help but wonder, if there is something more, an ulterior motive, God has for my life?

During these years of growing our family and being involved in various outreaches, we attended a local non-denominational New Testament type fellowship of likeminded believers. We enjoyed the family-like connection and fellowship there. Biblically based spiritual truths were taught well and we grew *in grace and in the knowledge of our Lord and Savior Jesus Christ. To him be the glory both now and forever. Amen (II Peter3:18)*.

Our investment of love, time, and commitment there paid back many dividends throughout the years. We are still reaping benefits from our time of twenty-four years there. As God has called us to be "pilgrims in this land," we eventually followed a new season in our lives and traveled northward to another fellowship. During this season of change, our boys became men, had some excellent mentoring with a youth group and its leaders, and then branched out to their own lives and careers.

It was time to pack up and move to the next pilgrimage, another local fellowship our daughters introduced us to. This time, it was southward. This fellowship is where Iris and I first met. We became active there, singing in the worship band and the Hubs doing children's ministry. Realizing our season was ending after several years there, we transitioned for a short time eastward. I was in a spiritually dry season and needed to retreat for a time; the Hubs attended a church for a while, but it wasn't a good fit.

We began the search for a place of refuge, of spiritual safety, a place where we could be free to sit at Jesus' feet, a place of acceptance and a place of worship, a place to hear the Word of God preached without apology and have fellowship with other believers. Hubs needed to be in outreach ministry, as this is his life's calling, his gift. I needed fellowship, and sisters in the Lord. We looked westward and found our safe place; our refuge from the cares and intensity of life.

God commands us to go out and share His great love. Our job as believers is to share the Gospel, to bring others with us to the Kingdom of God. It is proclaimed in **Acts 1:8: "ye shall be witnesses unto me both in Jerusalem, and in all Judea, and in Samaria, and unto the uttermost part of the earth."**

What seemed like "disappointment" with churches we had departed from was actually our "appointment" with direction from Almighty God for us to fulfill His will and purpose in spreading the Gospel to our world. We had gone North and South, East and West in our pilgrimage and obedience to be where God wanted us for a time and season.

All the special friendships we made, people we ministered to, people who loved and accepted our family, would prove to be divinely intersected in our lives for a reason. A very special and profound connection: It would come to be our lifeline.

Seasons come and go; life takes us on paths we probably would have hidden from if we had been aware of the direction we were headed, the storms that were currently brewing and those that still lay ahead.

Ecclesiastes 3:1-8

To everything there is a season

and a time to every purpose under the heaven:

A time to be born and a time to die;

a time to plant, and a time to pluck up that which is planted;

A time to kill, and a time to heal;

a time to break down, and a time to build up;

A time to weep, and a time to laugh;

a time to mourn, and a time to dance;

A time to cast away stones and

a time to gather stones together;

A time to embrace, and a time to refrain from embracing;

a time to get, and a time to keep, and a time to cast away;

A time to rend, and a time to sew;

a time to keep silence, and a time to speak;

A time to love, and a time to hate;

a time of war, and a time of peace.

Chapter Fourteen: Storms

We soon found out a tempestuous storm system was brewing for two of our married daughters. We were aware of some issues but praying that all would right itself for them and the family. One marital storm blew, then the other. I am not going to tell their stories; suffice it to say that both marriages ended. We fully supported their decision to divorce. This dealt a nasty blow to our family; it rocked us to the core, causing us to fully understand the magnitude and consequence divorce inflicts on its recipients. While our goal and intent was to offer moral and spiritual support (as well as financial, if needed) and assist with the grandchildren involved, we were amazed how the hand of God made every provision for relocation, housing, schooling, and jobs. As we navigated the storms of divorce and recovery, the endless court documentation and proceedings, we held fast to our faith and offered emotional support as it was wanted and needed. We were so very thankful for faithful praying and trusted friends. The Grace and Mercy of our loving and caring, compassionate Heavenly Father continues to astound and humble me. There are just times in our lives when we *need* someone to **bear ye one another's' burdens (Gal. 6:2).**

I would love to write a fairy tale ending to the broken marriages, how God changed hearts and mended and restored relationships, but that was not the case. Both daughters accepted their part in the outcome and began new lives. One is currently going back to school to finish her degree.

The other daughter…well, this is where "Mourning Song" was born into being an extension of our **testimony.**

After re-locating to her hometown, our "other daughter" (who will be called Daughter in the remainder of our story) started over. She established her home, began to blossom, be herself, and to find her true self again. While we grieved the loss of her marriage, we maintained respect, civility, and kindness toward her former husband, the father of her two wonderful children.

Remember that verse that keeps resonating with my spirit? The one out of **Romans 8:28… "and we know that all things work together for good to them that love God, to them are the called according to His purpose."** Even in adversity, even with broken relationships, broken marriages, hurting hearts, and children who are caught between parents and visitation rights, torn between divided loyalties for their parents, EVEN in all these circumstances, God will work good out of the messes we make in our lives.

Hidin'...........

Monday, July 2, 2012

I wanna be an ostrich,
hide my head in the sand

look up oncet in a while,

duck back down a'gin.

Life can be stormy,

windy and rough

if'n you have Faith,

Love is Enough

To weather the storms and

winds of life... it'll see you through

in the midst of strife....

when the waters rage, get too deep

His Love will carry you, it will Keep

Holding us together, hanging on

His hands will catch us, like wings of a Dove

to the Promised Land, Far above....to

the gates of Glory, Streets of Gold...

There to sing Praises, and never grow old.

***

My family is proof positive. We have stood firm in our faith, believed the Word of God and His Promises, and taken it to the spiritual bank for investment in Heaven. We have yet to be tried in the fire of adversity of life like what storm is on the horizon.

Chapter Fifteen: Hell Unleashed

Daughter meets man at work. Daughter thinks he is wonderful. Dating ensues. Flowers, cards, romance, she is starry-eyed. They go on family outings with her kids. Family meets man; we are reserved, guarded. Advice to proceed with caution is barely heard; she allows more dating. They marry. We accept him into our family dynamics. He is absent some, excuses himself from family gatherings. Time marches on, they move to a different neighborhood, remodel a home; we visit and have family time, reservedly hopeful they will make a good team.

A couple years pass, and their marriage disintegrates.

They divorce. It is ugly, costly, and sometimes acrimonious. She just wants to be done, to move on from this emotional, spiritual, expensive mistake in judgment. She sells the home, packs up and begins looking for a place to start over - again.

The week before on April 27, 2017, Hubs read a passage that spoke intimately to him, a verse that blessed and encouraged him as he prayed earnestly over a ministry outreach in which he was working:

Let your steadfast love come to me, O Lord, your salvation according to your promise" (Psalm 119:41, New Standard Revised Version).

God's lovingkindness and tender mercies are new—and real—every day. The Lord was sending an extra portion of His steadfast love to us, before we would desperately need it. A lifeline, tossed out with tender loving care, ready for us when we needed to grasp it as we were about to sink into the depths of heartache and grief.

While the family was out of town on a campout, the grand kids with their father, Daughter's Mama on a grandma mission in Alabama, Mama gets a phone call. "Have you talked to Daughter today?" "No, I saw her last night; we don't usually call each other every day." I was informed of a tragic incident in the area Daughter lived.

Mama checks news. There is serious danger, trouble, and trauma. Mama can't find anything out, calls Daughter's neighbor, a trusted friend. It is confirmed: Daughter has been shot and killed, left on the side of the road.

In shock, but have to take care of her children, make necessary calls, to family, figure out how do I DO this? NOTHING IN MY LIFE HAS PREPARED ME TO BE CALM IN THE MIDST OF MURDER AND BE STRONG FOR MY FAMILY!

Once we knew for certain what had happened, my son, his wife and I did valiantly in ministering to each other as we grappled with the awfulness of this news. We were thrown into a severe state of shock. One of our "Spiritual First Responders" was a precious saint of God from Wetumpka, Alabama, Pastor Mike from Wellspring Community Church. This is where our son and his family attended church. He came quickly to render first aid to our torn asunder hearts and souls. He loved on us and prayed with us, offered comfort and just stayed with us as we processed and wept.

Meanwhile, back at our home, family returned from their trip and others gathered with Hubs to give support and comfort to our family there. They stayed with my family, filling in the gap until emotions settled. We will always be eternally grateful for this gentle and loving expression of care and concern. We make it through the night. Hubs and a dear family friend travel the next morning to get me. In shock, mind numb as I try to comprehend what and how, why this has happened. The grands are at my home when I arrive. We grieve together. Investigation is ongoing. Family and friends rally around us. From the North, to the South, from the East and West, friends and loved ones come to grieve, hug, encourage and support us while we try to make sense of this senseless tragedy.

My baby daughter, mother of two wonderful children, murdered at 38 years of age, in the prime and beauty of her life. My girl, who loved life and adventure, who was a beautiful soul and person and friend and daughter: gone. Just "poof" and a bullet had taken her breath, her existence, her life—away.

Chapter Sixteen: Mourning Song

Consider the lowly Whippoorwill. It is not a beautiful bird; it has natural colorations that blend in with its wooded habitat. One could easily ignore this unassuming, camouflaged creature, if one could even spot it in the landscape. Some would call it an ugly bird. However, when it opens its mouth to sing, what a melody! It gives me pause, makes me want to imitate its sound. And my soul resonates with its song, a song of soulful mourning, of loneliness. It trills, tentative at first, then more insistent, while it is waiting for a return call from its mate. It chants its song, repeatedly "Whip-poor-will! Whip-poor-will!"

The whippoorwill song...is a mournful, lonely sound; its trilling in the dusky late evening as the sun goes down, wafting off the cool night breeze. The whistles, trills and wills of its melodic chirring was as if calling for a soulmate to answer, or a friend to nestle down in the damp grass for the upcoming night, for companionship.

After Daughter moved away from home for her first professional job, we would share the sounds of spring with each other, and whoever heard the first whippoorwill song of the season would call the other. It became something we both looked forward to sharing; a special moment between Mother and Daughter, a connection of nature that we both enjoyed. I listened closely for them to show up in the night twilight of early spring to hear their calling, their trilling across the pasture and through the trees.

Late in the evening, I heard one close by our barn. I hurried to set my phone on record and captured a great sound bite of its song. This was edited into my phone sounds and became Daughter's ring tone on my phone! I sometimes got confused if I was outside late; she would call, I would not answer because it sounded so real, I couldn't distinguish between the two!

Now, I listen more intently for their mournful song in the spring. It is a private mourning melody for me, as I breathe deeply, letting the sorrowful sounds bathe and soothe my soul as I remember and miss my lovely Daughter. I imagine she hears it in heaven, understanding and loving me from afar, from the glories of her heavenly home. It is, in some unexplainable way, a message of comfort, to hug and love on me, to say she is ok, and is where she longed to be, her eternal place of worship to the King of Kings, her Savior and Lord.

The Lord uses foolish things of the world to confound the wise; and makes beautiful things out of ashes.

Isaiah 61:1-3

The Spirit of the Lord God is upon me;

because the Lord hath anointed me

to preach good tidings unto the meek;

he hath sent me to bind up the brokenhearted,

to proclaim liberty to the captives,

and the opening of the prison

to them that are bound;

To proclaim the acceptable year of the Lord,

and the day of vengeance of our God;

to comfort all that mourn;

To appoint unto them that mourn in Zion,

to give unto them beauty for ashes,

the oil of joy for mourning,

the garment of praise for the spirit of heaviness;

that they might be called trees of righteousness,

the planting of the Lord,

that he might be glorified.

As I swing in the late evening breeze, the sounds I love to hear are close by: crickets chirping, a bat whisking overhead, the owl in the distance, hooting its deep sounds, the world quieting, settling, for peaceful slumber, for a few blessed hours of rest for our weary souls. Then, the "whippoorwill" trills. It is insistent, over and over again, as its mate assures the other with a responding "whippoorwill" of its own.

I sigh with longing, an ache in the depths of my soul, where sorrow burrows deep. I remember Daughter, her laugh, love for life and family, her love for the Lord, her sense of adventure, her fun-loving personality.

And I mourn, grieve, sigh, and sometimes, shed a few tears, so God can add them to His vessel.

WHY, GOD...WHY? WHO?

WE WERE NOT READY FOR THIS TO HAPPEN, NOW OR LATER! We were blindsided by this vicious act against our daughter.

The storm had come in full fury, like a hurricane, hovering over us, relentless and angry, unleashing its full force of evil energy into our existence.

And yet, there was an abiding (calm) PEACE—an assurance in our souls—as we had to navigate planning her funeral and legalities of closing her home, caring for her children and relocating them to their father. Most of this is a blur in my mind;

how we managed to get through the first week after her death was simply by putting one foot in front of the other and functioning because we had to. Our family rallied and circled the proverbial wagons as the shock faded into reality. We fully understood the context of what we were now facing.

In the multitude of counselors there is wisdom, and after consulting with the funeral director, we met with Daughter's pastor and ours to plan her service. Who, what, when and where, as well as the how was discussed. Granddaughters formulated a music playlist and video picture memorial for the guests, family and friends who would attend. Service and speakers were assigned. All the arrangements were a huge emotional weight looming large over us. So unexpected, so tragic, so unimaginable that we were preparing to bury our youngest daughter: a mother, sister, and friend of many. Nothing we had experienced in our lives prior to this could have readied us for this emotionally traumatic journey.

I did know one thing about her service that was paramount: that everything spoken, everything sung, every little detail was to **GLORIFY THE LORD**, not any person. As a family we were united in one thought about this:

Neither give place to the devil. Let him that stole steal no more (Ephesians 4:27,28a).

Genesis 50 relays the story of Joseph, how he reacted to his brothers after they had sold him into slavery, and as the Lord would care for his own, Joseph spoke to them: "ye thought evil against me, but God meant it unto Good, to bring to pass as it is this day, to save much people alive."

This is what we mean when God would be glorified, that we would not give the enemy any further place to kill, steal and destroy, but God would receive Glory and Praise through and in spite of our pain and grief, our difficult and broken path through the valley of the shadow of Daughter's death.

What the enemy meant for evil, to destroy our daughter, her family and ultimately, ours, along with our testimony, would not have any bearing on the spiritual significance of her last testimony. The Lord would—and did—have the last word on the matter!

The service was everything we had hoped for, and then so much more. We thought of our family, relatives, friends, work associates, and considered how many would attend; we guessed 200 or so. After the services, one of our pastors reported back that there were close to 700 in attendance. That's a lot of hugs and comfort! We didn't have enough time to personally receive everyone in attendance, but those who came understood the restraints of scheduling and time. They gathered as one unified army of support, shielding, praying, and protecting our wounded and grieving family. Close friends and others surrounded us, supporting and loving and caring for every need. We felt secure, as if wrapped in Grandma's thick and comforting quilt, each person there a piece that was fashioned and sewn together for such a time as this.

Words do not do justice to the security and overwhelming, abiding love and care, the solace, we experienced that day.

After a very powerful, spiritually uplifting service, we followed Daughter and the entourage of family and friends to the cemetery. This last time of goodbye will be forever etched in our memories. The weather was perfect; the air was filled with a hushed, holy silence as we commended her, our Daughter, into the earth. "To be absent from the body is to be present with the Lord," when you are a person of faith, and she was. It was a very precious, very somber service. We lingered, comforting each other, just being there, being loved and cared for by all in attendance.

There is Hope in the Lord. With many assurances from His Holy Word, we were comforted, strengthened, sustained, and fortified to carry on.

After returning to the church for a meal, we continued to be cared for and loved on. Some who had traveled great distances needed to return to their homes. Others lingered for a time and eventually we all faced the inevitable: time to go home, rest, and begin to return to some semblance of life and schedules. Of course, that is easier to say than actually do!

From this time and into forever, Daughter would not come for a visit, hug her precious children, sing them sweet melodies of a lullaby, read them a story, or share in the thrill of the first whippoorwill song of spring. Her siblings would never be able to tease her, share their lives and accomplishments as they had been accustomed to. Her Dad would never get another sweet hug, her Mother never hear cherished words of "Hi, Mom...I love you!" Her children would never be able to call out for "Mama!" They would never know or hear her comforting voice of reassurance and encouragement or call their name. EVER.

Her song, her voice, her personhood, had been silenced.

Our Journey ... A Public Statement

As most of you know by now, we lost our Anna Louise in a most tragic and untimely death. We are devastated, broken... shattered. She was buried this past Saturday, resting beside her maternal grandmother, in a quiet, secluded country cemetery.

We did not know how to do this...there is no formula, no script that ever prepares a Mama and Daddy (and siblings and her children) to face the unthinkable. How do we grieve our baby girl, plan her funeral, and greet the many hundreds of people whose life she touched—our family has touched—through the years?

We did not have the fortitude or strength within ourselves. Because we are people of Faith, our Lord and Savior and Comforter came to our rescue! The Lord God showed Himself Mighty on our behalf, and surrounded all of us in His Love, Care and Shelter. Our family and friends rose up like a mighty army, taking care of our every need, whether it was food, kitchen supplies, tea, ice or just genuine heartfelt tears and hugs. We have described it as a "tsunami" of God's provision and care, enveloped in His tender love and mercy.

Anna was a woman of faith: we wanted to honor her, and above all, bring Glory to God even in the midst of her untimely death, that God would receive all praise, and His name magnified. That is just exactly what The Lord in His Divine Grace and Mercy allowed us to do. He was, without any doubt, the focus of Anna's service.

We continue through this valley, trusting God in all things and with all our loved ones. It will not be an easy journey. We will persevere and be conquerors in Christ.

We will be forever grateful to all of you who have showered us with this protective care and concern, provision of every need and extravagant love.

In Jesus' Name

Stephen and Sue Brown and families
May 10, 2017

***

While still in an altered state of shock and disbelief, grief and mourning, we had jobs, schedules, families that needed attention. We also had the almost unbearable responsibility of closing her home and disposing of household effects. Uppermost in the family's hearts and minds was that of loving and helping her children through the coming days and weeks and months and years of being motherless.

Because of the sensitive nature of these events, suffice it to say that we did everything in our power to be considerate of the children. We struggled through those days and weeks of intensity by the strength, grace, mercy and compassion of the Lord, buoyed by the support of loved ones and friends who walked along side us, offering love, assistance, protection and care.

For those of you who did this for our family, we are forever grateful.

***

Psalms 34:15 -18a states that "The eyes of the Lord are upon the righteous, and his ears are open unto their cry. The face of the Lord is against them that do evil, to cut off the remembrance of them from the earth. The righteous cry and the Lord heareth, and delivereth them out of all their troubles. The Lord is nigh unto them that are of a broken heart."

We had every confidence the Lord was hearing our cry, our brokenness, and would bring hope, healing and help in His time, in His way. His Word states that he *will store our tears in a bottle (Psalms 56:8).*

There will come a day when *God shall wipe away all tears from their eyes, and there shall be no more death, neither sorrow, nor crying, neither shall there be any more pain; for the former things are passed away (Revelation 21:4)*. That, my friend, is a day we are longing for, looking toward, to be re-united with all our loved ones who have gone before because they trusted Jesus as their personal Lord and Savior.

One evening I was watching *Anne of Green Gables*. There is a line in the movie that I was compelled to write down. This line absolutely describes our feelings and especially mine, as we navigated this valley of grief. Anne states, *"I have this deep dull ache and I really need to be alone to find my tears."* Public tears were few and far between for some of us. God had to get a much larger earthenware vessel just to store all the tears that were shed. I jest to lighten the mood, however, privately, the tears still flow, and the dull ache of sorrow is a constant reminder of losing Daughter.

Sorrow burrows deep.

During the ensuing days after Daughter's homegoing service, various affairs were tended to and the children were settled with as much care and love as possible. We see them frequently, and always enjoy their company. They are sweet and precious offspring, reminders of their mom's gracefulness, spirit of adventure, and happy go lucky personality.

Husband and I were reading through the book of Isaiah during this time of mourning. We were often stunned and amazed at the powerful reminders of God's care and His power to sway and change hearts, countries, and people. It would prove to be very spiritually timely as we read through to the end. Oh, that we could only grasp the love and compassion He wants His people to have! If we could only learn to completely trust the Lord! His Word, the Bible, brought us much hope and comfort during these difficult days. It continues to do so.

Jeremiah 29:11: For I know the thoughts that I think toward you, saith the Lord, thoughts of peace, and not of evil, to give you an expected end. Then shall you call upon me, and ye shall go and pray unto me, and I will hearken unto you. And ye shall seek me, and find me when you shall search for me with all your heart.

Proverbs 3:5, 6: Trust in the Lord with all thine heart; and lean not unto thine own understanding. In all thy ways acknowledge him, and he shall direct thy paths.

Isaiah 55:8, 9: For my thoughts are not your thoughts, neither are your ways my ways, saith the Lord. For as the heavens are higher than the earth, so are my ways higher than your ways, and my thoughts than your thoughts.

Isaiah 26:3: Thou wilt keep him in perfect peace, whose mind is stayed on thee: because he trusteth in thee.

As our families resumed schedules, jobs, family life and other activities, whatever "normal" had been was profoundly disrupted for all of us. The dynamics of what had been were very different now. Nothing would ever be as it was; our worlds were turned upside down and inside out by one vicious act of cowardice.

We continued; sometimes simply by plodding on, one foot in front of the other, just to navigate our very changed lives. This journey, through the valley of the shadow of death, was new territory, one we had to depend on the Lord to help us propel forward. I think of Christian in *Pilgrim's Progress*, and the path he embarked on, the dangers he faced, the turmoil he experienced. How he came to depend on the Lord to make it to the end of his journey. We are very much like that; this world is not our home, we are pilgrims traveling through a rough and weary landscape, with a goal of heavenly reward!

We read Psalm 23 now and it has more spiritual depth and meaning than ever before. The Lord truly is our Shepherd.

Psalm 23

The Lord is my shepherd;

I shall not want.

He maketh me to lie down in green pastures:

he leadeth me beside the still waters.

He restoreth my soul:

he leadeth me in the paths of righteousness

for his name's sake.

Yea, though I walk through the valley of the shadow of death,

I will fear no evil:

for thou art with me;

thy rod and thy staff they comfort me.

Thou preparest a table before me in the presence

of mine enemies:

thou anointest my head with oil;

my cup runneth over.

Surely goodness and mercy shall follow me

all the days of my life:

and I will dwell in the house of the Lord forever.

Tryin' to.....

February 13, 2018

Tryin' to overcome
Sorrow and Heartache
Grief and Confusion
Brokenness and Questions
We have

It is an ongoing daily struggle to overcome all the issues
Of death, life, continuing without her. How do we go on?
How do we help her children grieve...we flounder in our tears,
our monotone response of life,
where there is no color, nor feeling, or deep
Enjoyment of coming Spring.

Where is hope...joy...peace...comfort...understanding
in the midst of conflicts of our hearts, our emotions...our being?
We don't sleep...we mull it over in our subconscious minds as we go
about
Putting one foot in front of the other, leaded feet, doggedly going thru
the motions, existing in life but not truly living?

We wear masks of "being ok," pressing in and on the life we are living.
Trying to be courageous in the face of our personal adversity:
The struggle is our life reality...

We are broken, fallen on knees
scraped with the depths of despair
bandaged with scars that don't heal
Our wounds.

So many questions.

And then, a whisper of Hope, and Touch by His Spirit, an Earth Angel
sent to Comfort and Console. A word of encouragement like
"Apples of Gold and leaves of Silver."

It is … Nourishment for our souls and hearts
Prepared by Father God and sent through His Word.
Timely delivered when we needed an uplifting word,
a Stream of refreshing for our Thirsty souls …
a balm of healing for our cracked and broken heart.
Still, quiet, healing waters washing over the hurt, confusion,
the not knowing…

Removing and covering the wounds
of heart and soul, mind and spirit
to Restore unto us the Joy of our Salvation,
the Hope of our high calling in Christ Jesus.

Delivering peace and calm to our Grieving families
To a place of retreat, acceptance of our selves,
Our feelings, our hopes, dreams and convictions.

Looking…always looking…upward and onward toward
Our Redeemer, Our Hope, Our Salvation…Our Eternal Reward.

To be with Him…and a joyous Reunion with her!

(Tryin' to… was written in a few moments of angst, turmoil and grief when I was broken hearted, burrowed under a blanket of grieving my daughter.)

***

Bolstered by our faith, encouraged by the support and care of friends and family, we lifted our chins and began piecing our lives back together. Finding our way, tentatively at first, the demands of living our lives, maintaining regular work and school schedules became the order of the day, sometimes of the hour. Settling in to our different normal was a challenge. We met the challenge head on! We persevered, knowing that our Heavenly Father was directing our steps, sheltering us under His wings, undergirding us with His Spirit, picking us up when we were weak, helping in our time of need, holding us in the right hand of His righteousness.

There was a void, an empty spot in our family where Daughter had been; when we gathered, chatted and shared, we all felt her absence. It would never be the same in our family without her.

Time passes along, ever so slowly; it does not heal all wounds. It does lessen the effects of them; takes the edge off. As we manage to have some semblance of normalcy and enjoy the holidays without her, the firsts of special occasions are the hardest to experience. Mother's Day, summer vacation, lazy days of school being out, Fourth of July, kids' birthdays, Thanksgiving, Christmas...Daughter's birthday: all of these, manageable, but filled with loss.

Anna...A Remembrance...

(Written as a tribute on the 1ˢᵗ anniversary of her death, April 30, 2018)

Anna Louise Brown, born December 31, 1978 in Cottage Hill, Florida, was taken from us on April 30, 2017, in Molino, Florida. She was a woman of Faith, having accepted Jesus Christ as Lord and Savior at a young age. Anna was a caring and compassionate person, helping others and ministering to them with God's Love and Grace. She never met a stranger, often smiling and greeting many with whom she came into contact.

As we reflect on her life, we remember a vivacious personality with a joy for living life to the fullest. She loved to ride horses, and experience the wind blowing through her hair and the sun shining on her face. She would often take a walk and wander through the woods to explore God's creation. She enjoyed running and participated in numerous charity runs as well as simply taking off for a long run in the evening to finish out her day. As a certified diver, she had gone on several underwater adventures. Her curiosity led her to travel to various locations where she met new people and kindled friendships.

Her desire to minister to others was manifested through her mission trips to Guatemala, the Samaritan's Purse Distribution center in Atlanta, Georgia, and locally with her Dad with Baptist Disaster Relief. She was involved in many activities with her church family, Hamilton Baptist Church in Robertsdale, Alabama, and had plans to go with them to Haiti. She participated in choir, sang solos, taught a Sunday School Class for College and Career adults, and helped in the nursery. Anna also ministered to others through her profession as a Physical Therapy Assistant. Truly having a gift for helping people feel better, her light shone through with many testimonials of how well she could work a patient; pressing them to do more than they thought possible, yet gently encouraging them that they could. In a note received by the family, a co-worker states, "Anna was a very special person. Her love for the Lord and people shone through every day. She was a blessing to all of her patients and us staff. Truly an inspiration!"

Daughter and I

Anna wrote the following when she was joining a class at her church:

"I am...doing life as a working, blessed Mom of two amazing children. The Lord has blessed me with a nice job in which I am able to work four days a week and still pay all of our bills and maintain our car. I love being a mom! There are moments and days and situations that are tough and rough and painful and challenging and hard; but the joy of loving and having the privilege to nurture and teach my kids is a gift. I know they are each God's first, and that helps me worry less when they are away. I work as a Physical Therapist Assistant...I love doing therapy! I have a great family. I have wonderful parents and I have a growing relationship with my Creator, my Lord, my salvation, my strength, provider, comforter and friend. With my natural family and my church family, I am never alone or separated. I receive love and support and physical, tangible help when it's needed. That support and encouragement makes single parenting not so single! Yay!"

Her epitaph reads:
PRECIOUS IN THE SIGHT OF THE LORD IS THE DEATH OF HIS SAINTS
PSALMS 116:15
(Tribute written with Christy Stevens)

Father and Daughter

Father, Daughter, Mother

Daughter and siblings

Chapter Seventeen: Another Crisis

As the first anniversary of her death was approaching, the family was preparing for a remembrance in her honor. We were also planning an annual family reunion, and several family members were coming in from out of town and out of state. Guests began arriving; some of them stayed in our home.

As these events were unfolding, drawing nearer, my personal anxiety was getting stronger, and I began having some health issues. I was having trouble focusing on conversations, struggling to form coherent sentences. Normally I am pretty articulate! I couldn't even walk a straight path to anywhere. I walked a crooked path, veering, staggering like a drunken person across the yard to my chicken house! My left side was droopy; my left leg was not responding, and my left arm not working correctly. I am left-handed, so when my writing ability was diminished that really alarmed me. I tripped UP my back porch steps one day, almost falling on my face. I couldn't comprehend what was happening to me! My lab work was perfect, with great cholesterol numbers and good blood pressure readings. I knew I hadn't had a stroke. I began walking to the left and hugging the center line when driving. This was so uncharacteristic of me, yet I was confused about what was going on.

After muddling through the company and activities associated with the reunion, I just wanted to sleep, rest, and do nothing for a while. After all the guests were gone my oldest daughter insisted I see my doctor. There had to be an organic, physical reason for these behaviors. I dutifully scheduled an appointment; they were able to get me in quickly when I described the symptoms. He performed an eye-hand coordination test; I failed. An MRI was scheduled, and the doctor was kind enough to stat the orders. During the MRI (which was ordered without contrast), I was sure they weren't gonna find anything. After all, I WAS under a lot of stress, and I really thought it would just...get better. Halfway through the MRI the tech came in and said they needed to give me contrast. I knew then they had found something. I didn't know what to think, I couldn't comprehend the possibilities, as they were too terrible. I had already lost several friends from brain cancer; I couldn't fathom it happening to me, not now, not here, not after what our family had been through! Finally, I was released from the noisy machine, gathered my things and Hubs drove us home.

The tech had told me the doctor would call later in the afternoon with the results. Testing was done at 8 am; he called before noon. April 24, 2018 was the day I was diagnosed with a "benign meningioma" brain tumor. I was alone when the doctor called with the results. I solemnly listened, confirming I had understood. Hubs was in his shop, which is on our property, so I walked to him, wrapped my arms around him and sobbed the

72

news. I very deliberately stated to him, "We are going into a fight for my life." And yes, I was broken, shocked and sad that our world, my future, would once again be threatened with a crisis of epic proportions.

As we processed this shocking news, considered the impact, planned how to tell all who needed to know, weighed our different medical options, we cried out once again for divine intervention. My primary care physician referred me to a new (to Pensacola) neurosurgeon. They called and scheduled an appointment for consultation, and another clearer, more precise MRI. Having to tell my family was the second hardest thing we have had to deal with in less than a year. As I reflect on these days and few short weeks leading up to surgery, I remember it being surreal, foggy as I just got through each day.

Chapter Eighteen: Heaven...I Can Only Imagine

Wednesday, May 9, 2018, after my second MRI
We are having to meet another crisis—head on—with concern and faith mixed together in a jumble of hurried appointments, hoops jumping and all kind of interesting, challenging events!

Hubs took me to the "stat" appointment, which is my second MRI in a few days. As I waited, I rested...with my eyes closed. Thought of many things, but mostly, about my family, how this was impacting them, and the concerns for the younger ones who might not quite understand the situation. Then, I was called back, "Number forty-one!!" I left the waiting area and followed the technician.

As I prepared myself, and went to the "monster roaring machine," I selected the music for my "listening pleasure" even though the monster with a sliding mouth is louder than a freight train! I chose a nature theme; that should soothe me and make me calm, right? Well bless Pat, it didn't! Too somber! They finished the no contrast and injected me with contrast. Oh, by the way, I told techie guy, could ya' change to worship and praise for me? That was done, and I was put into monster mouth again. The first song was one I did not recognize, I could only hear snippets of it, as the monster was grumble-y. Then, without explanation or understanding what was happening...

I started weeping! Where did this come from, I asked myself? I was warm, cozy and secure in My Father's Love, wrapped up in a blanket of His Care. My spirit heard it first, my mind second, and I cried softly as I wrapped my mind and soul around "I Can Only Imagine." What a powerful song! As I worshiped the Lord, my heart—grief—traveled to thoughts of Anna and what she was rapturously experiencing. Soon, the MRI was done, and I could escape that noisy "thang." Techie Guy said, "you did great!" And I did, all things considered. As I got up, I shared.

"I cried; when that worship song came on, I couldn't help but consider what it was like, to be in heaven and worship and praise Jesus. We lost a daughter last year, her murder unresolved, and that song is so helpful!!"

He smiled at me, didn't say a word, then escorted me back to the changing area, and gave me directions to exit. I don't know if I impacted him or not...only God knows. I must be obedient, to share Jesus' Love with my world.

A word fitly spoken is like apples of gold in pictures of silver (Prov 25:11).

Be encouraged: A word spoken to an unsaved person...a person who is hurting, a stranger...is a word of encouragement that they—and you—need to hear you speak!

***

Exactly one week before I was diagnosed, Hubs and I read and claimed this passage:

II Corinthians 1:20: For all the promises of God in him are yea, and in him Amen, unto the Glory of God by us.

We relied on this verse for encouragement, comfort, when we couldn't understand the whys of our lives being disrupted and turned topsy-turvy, upside down and inside out. Could a God whom we served, WOULD a God whom we loved and was submitted to, put us through such crisis? How dare He, you might ask. We had been through a very dark valley losing Daughter. That valley was and is still in front of us, we are still trudging along, not yet out of the shadows of her death.

Chapter Nineteen: Consult Time!

We had three going into the appointment, Hubs, oldest daughter, Christy, and I. We sat, anxious to find out results from the latest MRI and to hear what the neurosurgeon would recommend. After getting the preliminaries out of the way and finding my blood pressure was slightly elevated (I wonder why...doctor visits seem to affect me that way), the doctor came in. She put us at ease immediately, and began explaining what I had, and that it needed to be removed sooner than later. We viewed the MRI results, astonished at the size of the tumor. It was about the size of a hard ball, 6 cm in diameter! We asked questions and gathered facts; other things were discussed that I have no recollection of.

I sat there; half listening to her recommendations, my mind whirling as I thought about how this would impact my two grandchildren that had so recently lost their Mama. How could God let this happen? Why in the world do we have to deal with this traumatic diagnosis so soon after losing Daughter? Why, God, why? I tried to listen, to connect to the doctor. After getting as much information about my prognosis and treatment recommendations, she highly recommended not waiting too long. We asked for the weekend to process, plan, and tell family.

One of the options we considered was traveling to UAB (University of Alabama – Birmingham) to seek treatment. We had experienced good treatment with other family members there, and knew it was an excellent hospital. The downside to going there was the difficulty in not having family close by and serious travel concerns for many follow up appointments. We just couldn't wrap our heads around the excessive physical and emotional strain it would put on the whole family.

We regrouped at home, discussing what to do along with time frame for surgery. We wanted to schedule as soon as possible, because symptoms were getting more intense. All three of us felt peace and confidence in using this doctor. We believed she was the right surgeon for my situation.

Prior to our consult appointment, I had read a bio of hers. She came highly regarded from another location in Florida, had seventeen years of experience and a specialty in my particular type of tumor, meningioma. She had been head of the department of Neurosurgery as well, and just re-located to Pensacola and established her office—get this—six short weeks before I needed her expertise! We sensed in our spirits that she was sent here by God for such a time as this...my hour of need. Does God provide for His own or what? That still gives me chill bumps when I consider how God showed Himself mighty on our behalf! He gave us favor with the doctors and scheduling, even providing an excellent, experienced, specialized surgeon for my journey!

For the eyes of the Lord run to and fro throughout the whole earth, to show himself strong(mighty) in the behalf of them whose heart is perfect (devoted) toward Him... (II Chronicles 16:9).

After our appointment on Friday morning, Hubs and I left early Saturday morning for a short retreat to my Dad's farm. He is elderly and this is the kind of news that I didn't want to share with him over the phone. Several family members live in the area, so we could also tell them in person. There was a scheduled workday at the farm, so it would give us busy work and not just time to overthink our crisis. We were able to chat without distraction on the trip up and back. It was enjoyable in the sense that we were able to just get away and clear our heads, spend some time together, view some spring scenery along our route and reconnect with family. We relaxed and made the best of the difficult circumstances we were confronting.

Our minds were made up: we would stay in town for the surgery. It would be such a hardship on our immediate family to have me out of town for the procedure. The concern meter would have burst through the top if they couldn't be with me! Our decisions complete, we made the return trip with utmost confidence in our future. Monday morning after our trip, we called the Neurosurgeon's office to schedule the appointment. I asked for three weeks, the Monday after Mother's Day. She was gracious and consented to my request. She had initially told us, "As soon as possible." It was imperative to act quickly. It was up to the Lord to guide the surgeon, protect and heal his child, and help the family be faithful to Him in the midst of this danger.

What time I am afraid, I will trust in thee (Psalm 56:3).

I will be honest here; I was gravely concerned for my welfare. I do believe my adult kids were as well. I was spiritually ready to meet my Maker, but I couldn't shake the feeling that I had something more to do here, something significant to offer the world. I say that humbly without pride. God was not finished with me here; I needed to get well so I could keep doing the things I do for the kingdom of God!

I wanted to thoroughly enjoy Mother's Day celebration, not just for myself, but for my daughters and daughters-in-love and grandchildren. On Mother's Day, Andrew, my youngest son pranked me with a goofy gift. When I unwrapped the present, there was a bag of marbles and a multi-head screwdriver. I knew immediately what they meant: the marbles were to replace any the surgeon would take out, (Need I explain? You know, he was insinuating I would lose my marbles). The screwdriver was to tighten up loose screws in my head! That boy! It made me laugh; it was a good stress reliever.

(The marbles were added to my collection, the screwdriver is an ornament on my dresser, and I use it now when I need a break from stress. It is an easy way to get comic relief.

And I do have titanium plates and screws in my head as a result of the surgery technique used, so he was right on target and.... so very thoughtful. Yes, I have been asked if I needed to use the screwdriver a few times.)

In the event that something unforeseen happened, I didn't want Mother's Day celebrations of the future tainted with a bad memory. (Just the day after). Sick humor, I know. But these were my thoughts at the time. We were in waiting mode for surgery day. Staying busy was imperative to not thinking too much about it.

Our biggest concern was telling two of the grandkids. They had lost their mama the year before. Such agony of spirit I endured! How would they receive the news that their grandma (they call me Maw-maw) could be in jeopardy! Honesty is always the best policy, especially in matters of the heart. Questions flooded my mind as I prayed and sought wisdom and discernment in what and how I told them. The two grands were visiting for the coming Mother's Day weekend, and I had to tell them of my impending health crisis and surgery. I really didn't know what I was going to say or how to say it.

God's Grace and Mercy came through as He gave me a gentle way to tell them. They received the news, asked questions; one of them asked me the hardest question, "Maw-maw, are you going to die?" I gulped, quickly prayed for wisdom, and replied, "No, I am not. I am going to be okay." Once they got reassurances that God was in control, they ran off to play and process their thoughts.

Later, after they had gone to play, Christy confronted me. "Mom, you don't know that!" I looked her in the eye and replied, "I don't know it for sure, *but I could not tell that child it was a possibility." In my mind it was a little white lie; but in my heart and spirit, I felt calm. It was spoken more as a statement of hope and faith that it just had to be so.*

While I was waiting for my surgery date to get closer, I had been prescribed a steroid to take two times a day. There was swelling around the tumor that needed to be relieved and reduced before surgery. The downside to this medication was sleeplessness. I was faithful to take it, but I did have issues with lack of sleep. I read a lot, scrolled on various on-line sites, and did some online shopping since I was not able to drive. No fear; I didn't go crazy with the orders, just some basics I needed! Naps were a must during the day!

Our pastor had come for a visit the week before surgery, to share and encourage us, to pray with us, to bolster our faith before we went into this battle of medical warfare. We visited a good while, and then he shared a particular verse with us that we held fast to as we waited for surgery day to arrive.

The verse was Isaiah 41:10:

Fear thou not; for I am with thee: be not dismayed; for I am thy God. I will strengthen thee; yea, I will help thee, yea, I will uphold thee with the right hand of my righteousness.

Our pastor had just handed us a lifeline for the coming days and weeks we were facing. Incidentally, he was to finish a series in Nehemiah the following Sunday. The Lord had other ideas and redirected the sermon to this particular passage so the body of Christ at our local church could be encouraged and challenged with it as well! God is so good and loves us so much that He interrupts our plans to bring about a greater good for all of us! I'm glad we have a good pastor, one that cares for his people and most importantly, hears from the Lord!

One of the vital commands from scripture that we wanted to walk in obedience to was:

James 5:14, 15: Is any sick among you? Let him call for the elders of the church; and let them pray over him, anointing him with oil in the name of the Lord; and the prayer of faith shall save the sick, and the Lord shall raise him up; and if he hath committed any sins, they shall be forgiven him.

We did this very command. Not only did the elders come and pray, many of our church family circled around us like the wagon circling I spoke of earlier, lifting us up to the throne of God, beseeching Him on our behalf. What a powerful experience, what a force of love...surrounding us!

Chapter Twenty: My Garden of Gethsemane Morning

I remember distinctly rising early on Mother's Day morning. I was agitated and moody, stewing over what I was facing the next day. The steroids I was required to take didn't help my mood swings at all. After brewing a fresh pot of coffee, I walked outside, going to my swing to have a chat with the Lord. From my perspective, it was more like a "come to Jesus" meeting, and I am the one that had to change my attitude! As I sat enjoying the early morning world waking up, I felt deep anguish, and likened it to Jesus in the Garden of Gethsemane, as I faced my unknown future. I knew only I was facing surgery and wouldn't know the outcome until afterwards. We had been told the tumor most likely was not benign; the percentage was 95% sure it was cancerous. I prayed and beseeched the Lord, and even asked some very tough, hard questions of Him. I cried before Him on behalf of my wounded and heart-broken grandchildren. I cried out for mercy, healing, and compassion for our family. I cried out, not understanding the why's of everything, wishing "this cup could pass from me," and yet, knowing it was not going to. As the Lord listened to me, I felt in my spirit a calm encompassing my soul, an infusion and acceptance of His Love, Grace, Mercy, Compassion and Understanding washing over me. I had a special reassurance that His Spirit was with me, deep in my heart, my soul. Somehow, everything would be okay. It just HAD to be!

The last day of family time before my surgery was Mother's Day Sunday. I remember pastor telling me, as I was leaving church on Mother's Day, "to go home and enjoy your family." So, I did! It was a memorable, fun, and carefree day: perfect! We loved on each other, enjoyed good food, and great fellowship with extended family members who were visiting. It was a sweet, anointed day. Again, we felt the peace and love flowing freely among us, and from our Heavenly Father, sheltering us in his Love.

Chapter Twenty-one: Blessings Poured Out!

After the diagnosis, imminent surgery dates were set. Hubs went to the financial affairs office at the hospital to facilitate payment of the bill.   While we understood the surgery would not be "inexpensive," we were not prepared to hear the total anticipated cost of such an intense surgery and hospital stay. At the time, we had no insurance, as both of us had pre-existing conditions that made buying into a policy cost prohibitive. Through faith, and trust in God's provision, we had managed to be relatively healthy with a minimal of medical interventions, even while raising our large family.   When our case worker informed us of the cost, it took our breath away. It was stated to be hundreds of thousands of dollars, to be exact: in excess of $168,000. I have never seen that amount of money in all my life, and it was insurmountable to even consider paying that off in our lifetime. We prayed, "Lord, help...what do we do?" Hubs discussed various options with our case worker, and we could establish the ability to make monthly payments. We asked about a cash payout discount and were told there was a consideration for that; she would get back to us with information. When she finally called us back, the offer she gave was an astounding discount that would be extended over a period of time to make the payout transition palatable for our budget! As we negotiated payments with other offices, and told of the hospital discount, they matched or offered lesser discounts for the cash payment. What seemed impossible as we started out became very possible as God provided and met every need!

But my God shall supply all your need according to his riches in glory by Christ Jesus (Philippians 4:19).

As we moved forward and navigated preparations for surgery, the hospital stay and recuperation, the Lord was moving mountains on our behalf, showing Mercy and Favor for our finances. Two months after surgery, ALL the medical billings were paid off!!

Now, who but God can do such things as that?

There were sacrifices made on our part, and we became more diligent in our thrifty spending habits to compensate the family budget. We had a "house account," loosely speaking, to build our dream house in retirement. This account was largely depleted to ensure my health and well-being. After all, what good is a new house, without Wife, Mama, and Maw-maw to be there to care for all the family?

Our gratitude, thankfulness, and heart-felt "thank you" to all the people who co-operated with God's divine intervention and assisted to make this miracle happen!

We give all Glory to the Lord, for every miracle He has graciously provided for our family during all these difficult times. God is good; all the time, He is Good!

While looking for a medical statement several months after my surgery, I found the following handwritten statement on Hubs' desk. It grabbed my heart, made me pause and realize how my crisis had affected him, that he had written and expressed his thoughts about it in this way:

> She's lying in bed asleep. She does that now more than she used to. Her words have been crossed for years so we were not aware. If we corrected her she would retort, None of us knew. She did not know. Christy noticed she was walking leaning left and one day saw her driving crossing the center line a lot. Christy insisted we see a doctor. Doctor said get an MRI on the brain. We did. He called. We know. Why didn't we notice? Why were we so blind and deaf to what was right in front of us? We were all going on with life and death and love and service; Loving together, serving together, living together and facing death together. What's next? Visit a Neurosurgeon. This thing is 6 cm. Has it done permanent damage? How much time do we have? Can you do surgery? Will you get all of it? Are you the one for the job?
> There will be bills to pay. God will supply what we need. There will be mercy and grace. Surely goodness and mercy shall follow me all the days of my life. And I will dwell in the house of the Lord forever.

Chapter Twenty-two: Surgery Day

Hubs, Christy, and I arrived at the scheduled time, paperwork in hand. We were at the wrong area and had to be escorted to the right location. There had been a power outage, and the facility was currently running on backup generator power, but as I was checked in and called back to the pre-op area, all was up and running properly. Unbeknownst to me, there was a waiting room FULL of family and friends, gathered in support and love and prayer for this critical surgery.

Once again, family and friends gathered from the North and South, the East and the West, to love on us and pray and support us. People from around the world in different locations were praying for the best outcome possible. Our pastor had come to offer encouragement and prayer as well. I was ready to "get this show on the road," and was whisked off to the operating room.

Our expectations were for an eight-hour surgery, a five-day hospital stay, and an extended recuperation time at home. While I was deep into my sweet sleep on anesthesia, without a care in the world, my tribe was in the waiting room... waiting. I can't imagine what they were all thinking, processing, as the surgeon began her work on removing the tumor. All of us were immersed, bathed in heart-felt prayers before the throne of God, especially the medical team working on me.

We were told to expect the eight hours of surgery, anything less could mean difficulty or complications, but we would have regular updates. Around 12:45, there was a concerted prayer going up in the waiting room; Daughter-in-love had taken the young one downstairs and felt an urgent need to pray at the same time but didn't know it was going on upstairs! Unbeknownst to us, that was the same time labs were being processed by pathology. Reports came back to the Doctor it was benign!! A divine intervention and gift from our Lord: benign tumor!

At the four-hour timeframe, the doctor appeared, wanting to speak to Hubs and Christy. My girl sat frozen, not wanting to hear, as information had been told a shorter surgery would mean complications. She rallied, gathered herself, and bravely went to get whatever news the doctor had. It was good!! Surgery completed, tumor mostly removed, and I was headed to ICU for recovery! Apparently, the tumor was easily removed, and we were told "birthed itself" out of my head! There is a small section she could not remove, about two percent, as it was attached to my sinus vein and could be problematic, even life threatening, if she bothered that vein.

Talk about good news! There was some kinda rejoicing going on in the waiting room! Relief and Joy flooded my tribe as they could finally let their guard down and bask in the love, grace and mercy of the Lord on my behalf.

We had entered the hospital with faith and confidence that God was in control, yet Hubs was burdened, weighed down with concern. As friends and family quietly but jubilantly slipped out and went about their schedules, Hubs and two sons also departed for home. Hubs was in front, the boys were following him and as they exited the hospital, they tell me their Dad was walking tall, straight, shoulders back, as if he was walking on air! I jokingly referred to this story as Hubs levitatin' in the Lord! Such a weight had been lifted from his shoulders, and to see the Hand of God moving in his family on his wife's behalf was a very "uplifting" experience!

Medical team got me settled in ICU, and once I was awake enough, sent me downstairs for an MRI. Then it was back upstairs for getting me mobile and functioning. I was enjoying my post-surgical drowsiness. it had been a while since I had slept all night and would be longer before that happened again.

The pain wasn't too intense, I was actually surprised. Medications given to me for pain had an adverse impact on my system, and I was nauseated. Oops, they didn't want me to be upchucking anything, so anti-nausea meds were given. After two attempts with pain management, I requested only super strength Tylenol; that worked as long as we stayed ahead of the pain. Recovery was nice! Since I was the only patient for the time being, I got treated really well, and all the nurses were super sweet, efficient and patient! My progress was amazing, and I transitioned to the floor the next day. I was walking, making coherent conversation, and finding myself returning to normal. I wanted to walk around the floor, get myself going so I could go home! I was still cautious with my walking, but my leg was getting signals again! Within twenty-four hours I was walking laps on the floor, PT came in to monitor my progress and I did stair steps with assistance from the handrail; they were impressed and signed off for release. I still had hurdles to complete, with home health care and Diabetes management. They all came in, made their assessments, signed off, and I was ready to be released. One issue, though, the surgeon needed to sign off. Her PA came in, saw how well I was doing, and consulted with the neurosurgeon, who came in a while later, checked me out good and signed me out! I could go home! Forty-eight hours after brain surgery, and I was headed home to recuperate!

Not only was the surgery less time than anticipated, the hospital stay was much less!

To God be the Glory!!

Getting settled in at home was a good feeling. Of course, there were concerns, but family had gone to great lengths to prepare and organize my care. My sleeping chair was fluffed and prepared, bathroom facilities were in place for a medically needy patient, there was a physical therapy basket of goodies for me to work with, and a small bell, chairside, to ring if I needed anything.

We also got a couple pictures to send to the out of town grands who were waiting to see with their own eyes that their Mawmaw was gonna be okay. I was more than okay; I was on the road to recovery and wholeness. I couldn't be more grateful for the wonderful love, care, devotion and support of my tribe of family and friends. I was facing a three-month recovery, with very limited activity. What would I do for that long? Time would tell.

***

Dripping faucet?

A couple weeks after my surgery, the family had gathered to enjoy a meal together. I was propped up in my recliner, with my feet elevated, resting. There was lots of chatter, laughing and just everyday contented family sounds wafting through the house.

I heard water dripping so I stopped talking and listened to where the sound was actually coming from. It was, literally, in my head! I exclaimed, "Did y'all hear that, did ya' hear it?" All heads did a quick swivel toward me, and every face was registering an "I think she has gone loco" look. For real, there were sounds in my head just like a dripping faucet. One of them responded, "No, Mom, we don't hear anything." I was chagrinned, and just about thought myself crazy. Then I heard it again. I told them I was serious; there was a dripping faucet sound inside my head. Christy came over, put her ear to my head, and sure enough, she heard it too! Of course, Mom's head noises became a novelty, and everyone wanted to hear them. We did call the neurosurgeon's nurse to ask if this was "normal," and was told yes, some patients do experience that. Whew! At least I wasn't crazy!

From that moment on, for several weeks, the noises continued and changed cadence in my head. They progressed from drippy faucet sounds, to frog-like ribbets, and gurgling, swishy sounds. They also got loud enough that one could hear them across the room. THAT was very unnerving. They were so bad it woke me out of a deep sleep several times. I distinctly remember sitting in church one Sunday, and it started up with dripping, sloshing, and swishing sounds. I was so worried someone sitting near me would hear it and be startled by what they were hearing. I could barely tolerate all the various noises inside my head. It was worse than having my stomach growl in church.

It seems the tumor had compressed some brain tissue, and the space where the tumor was located needed time to reabsorb normal body fluids. Because of swelling in the brain prior to surgery, and lingering swelling after surgery, it needed to drain and leave the area. As it became less pronounced, the sounds migrated from the top of my head, to the top back, down the back and into the trunk. I could hear it travel. It was a freakish thing to hear and know and deal with. Fortunately, it didn't last too long, and all swelling is gone and things inside my head returned to normal. (I think).

We settled into a routine of sorts. Hubs returned to work, and school continued for those who were in classes. Stephenie had farmed her tribe out and came for a week to help, give her assistance and TLC to her mama. Everyone stepped up and gave 100% to my recovery. Church, family, and friends provided excellent food, so much so we had to coordinate deliveries and amounts to keep from overflowing the refrigerator.

We were overwhelmed with the goodness and outpouring of love from our family and friends, from our church family. So many blessings poured in we were almost not able to contain them! I considered the song from long ago:

Blessed be the tie that binds, Our hearts in Christian Love,
The fellowship of kindred minds Is like to that above.

I was scheduled for a follow up appointment with my surgeon after two weeks. During the second week, my left ankle started swelling, so I elevated and monitored fluid retention. We also checked my leg for hot spots, fever or swelling, there were none. I was more mobile and trying to walk about our yard at a careful pace by then. During our visit with the doctor, I casually mentioned my swollen ankle. She checked me over thoroughly, didn't feel or see any physical symptoms of a DVT (deep vein thrombosis, or blood clot in the leg), but ordered a STAT on an ultrasound just to be sure. Off we go to the lab for testing! During the ultrasound, the tech was super quiet, and finished up with this comment: "I can't let you leave the lab just yet; we have another doctor reading the results and you need to wait for that before you leave." She escorted me to a bench seat, propped my leg up and told me "don't move your leg." Well. Having had a DVT twenty years prior, I knew what was up! I also knew how risky it had been that I was walking around with that thing in my leg!

Processing one more medical event was tough! I was deflated, discouraged, at yet another setback! And again, asking the Lord why I was being dealt another nasty medical trauma! After some time, and consulting with a triage of my doctors, my primary care physician prescribed a blood thinner and sent me home, under strict orders to be careful and don't run any marathons or much physical activity! The blood clot was an eight-incher, and had any of it broken off, could have life threatening consequences. This just magnified how ***God was caring for and protecting me, providing safety in the midst of our struggles*** to get me well and back on my feet to the path of recovery.

Chapter Twenty-three: Shoulder Roll!

Most of my mobility returned in the first week post-surgery. One area of concern was my left arm. It was not responding like we wanted. It was sluggish and weak; it didn't receive signals from my brain. Because I am left-handed, this was disconcerting to say the least! I am so much "left-handed" minded I didn't know if I could even train myself to use the right hand for writing.

We began a physical therapy regimen to strengthen that particular group of muscles and nerves. My left hand wanted to curl up, similar to a stroke victim's hand. I continued to exercise, hoping for the best outcome. We were not seeing results. I was thinking how very grateful and blessed I was to recover what I had. Even if I didn't get back full function of my left arm, I was alive, in my right mind, could care for myself, and was at home with my loving and supportive family.

After my two-week check-up, Hubs and I were driving home. I reached for something in the console, when it hit me: my left shoulder had responded! I did it again, to be sure I wasn't imagining it, and it responded naturally! Praise the Lord!

The next evening was prayer meeting night at our church. I was so stoked about regaining that "rolling shoulder" motion, that as I walked in, I spoke to a group of ladies who were chatting. "Hey, look what I can do!!" Yes, I rolled my shoulder for them right in the back of the church!

They laughed, rejoiced with me, and we proceeded to have church! I was so elated to have full mobility in my arm again!

Chapter Twenty-four: Spiritual Warfare

We have recognized that as believers, we are in a constant spiritual battle of enormous proportions; we must be on guard. Satan wants to destroy and defeat any Christian. In Ephesians 6, we read about the armor of God which equips us for battle:

Ephesians 6:10-18

Finally, my brethren, be strong in the Lord, and in the power of his might.

Put on the whole armour of God, that ye may be able to stand against the wiles of the devil.

For we wrestle not against flesh and blood, but against principalities, against powers, against the rulers of the darkness of this world, against spiritual wickedness in high places.

Wherefore take unto you the whole armour of God, that ye may be able to withstand in the evil day, and having done all, to stand.

Stand therefore, having your loins girt about with truth, and having on the breastplate of righteousness;

And your feet shod with the preparation of the gospel of peace;

Above all, taking the shield of faith, wherewith ye shall be able to quench all the fiery darts of the wicked.

And take the helmet of salvation, and the sword of the Spirit, which is the word of God:

Praying always with all prayer and supplication in the Spirit, and watching thereunto with all perseverance and supplication for all saints...

We must put this on and keep it on. We must stand firm in our faith, without wavering, and rely on God's strength. Understanding that we will face resistance, we must **"be strong in the Lord and in the power of His might"** and be dependent on Him.

Philippians 4:13 says "I can do all things through Christ which strengtheneth me."

It is imperative that we Christians remain steadfast in our resolve to serve the Lord, to be obedient to Him. We have two weapons of warfare that are vital to our spiritual well-being, the Word of God and Prayer. Our family would have been a lost cause without appropriating these two weapons. We haven't waited for crisis to strike; we have been using them for years, as we grew in relationship with the Lord. We are still growing, still learning, how to navigate this life effectively for the Glory of God. We are weak, we cry out for mercy and grace. God comes through with Love, Compassion and Forgiveness when we fail Him, and we do.

The Lord has used our difficulties to build and grow our faith, our trust in Him. He has led us through troubled waters to bring himself Glory. We are learning to trust God in our crisis, our sorrow, our pain; in return, the Lord is tenderhearted, merciful and holds us up with His right hand of righteousness. He has prevailed; He gave life back to me, restored joy to my family and will receive all Glory and Honor and Praise for this miraculous gift!

I remember a day that our youngest son Andrew asked me: "Mom, what is the purpose of this life?" He was going to school, had teenage angst, working a job he didn't like, and was serious in his asking. As I prayed for a brief, yet good and true answer, I replied: "Son, the purpose of anything is to glorify the Lord."

I would face having to prove the truth of that statement out in my own life as I navigated these crises of life.

We have given ourselves permission to grieve and heal, emotionally, physically, and spiritually. We do take time off, to get away, to retreat and be by ourselves so that we can "find our tears" as Anne of Green Gables stated in the movie. There are times we just need to be alone, or to cluster as a family to feel grief, to share our sorrow, to share our innermost thoughts to our loved ones. The world can be overwhelming when one is grieving. Sights, sounds, a scent, or a song can trigger deep emotions. Grief is sneaky and is no respecter of persons. It can be quiet, or it can roar in our hearts and make us want to scream, shout, and fall on our knees in despair. We have done all of these, many times over, and will probably do them again at some point.

Chapter Twenty-five: Perseverance

Perseverance is a key component to maintaining some kind of normalcy when a family meets crisis on this collision course called life. One has to believe in something, or they will fall for anything. Our family is grateful our Hope in the Lord was secure. I shared with a friend, when she asked how we kept going; my response was simply, "We just put one foot in front of the other" and go through the motions until we can feel and connect again.

During a conversation with Bret, one of my nephews, he made the comment "Life is just one big Faith exam." He is so right; there are two ways to get to the end, to get your grade. One with a "pass" into the gates of heaven with eternal salvation, the other is "fail" and be eternally separated from God the Father. I choose life with Christ.

Almost two years to the day of our life being tilted askew, we are persevering, continuing to remember the wonderful person Anna Louise, our baby girl, was. Her memory and spirit are alive and well. We will see her again!

As for me, I am well. I am almost back to normal, enjoying life, family, church and gardening. I will be monitored by my team of physicians for some time, as there is a slight possibility the tumor could begin growing again. There are treatments for that in the event it does. In the meantime, we continue in faith; God is good all the time, and all the time, God is good. We will be faithful.

We can only share our story as we experienced it. We are not super spiritual; we are unassuming, normal everyday working-class people. We are sinners, saved by the grace and mercy of a loving and forgiving, compassionate God. Our desire is to walk in relationship with our Savior. We can't persuade or convince any one individual to do likewise. We can help to show them what worked for us, what path we chose to take by the grace of God.

Perhaps...just perhaps, one person will turn to Jesus Christ. Maybe, one person will receive help in their grief and pain. That is our point and purpose in sharing this difficult journey with you, our readers.

God so loved the world, that he gave his only begotten son, that whosoever believeth in him should not perish, but have everlasting life (John 3:16).

Sharing Hope in Jesus, Hope and Healing in someone's pain and sorrow, to lift them up, and give a reason of the hope that is within us, that is why we share.

II Peter 3:15: But sanctify the Lord God in your hearts: and be ready always to give an answer to every man that asketh you a reason of the hope that is in you, with meekness and fear.

Romans 8:28: For we know that all things work together for good to them that love God, to them who are the called according to his purpose.

II Chronicles 16:9a: For the eyes of the Lord run to and fro throughout the whole earth, to shew himself strong in the behalf of them whose heart is perfect toward him.

Joshua 1:9: have not I commanded thee? Be strong and of a good courage, be not afraid; neither be thou dismayed: for the Lord thy God is with thee whithersoever thou goest.

Chapter Twenty-six: Year of Favor

Just before the start of 2018, my daughter-in-love was seeking the Lord for a special verse and encouragement for the coming New Year. She had hoped this would happen by Jan 1st, but it did not come to her then. The Brown family had experienced the unexpected and sudden death of a daughter in 2017. All the family was traumatized by her death, especially her children.

Desiring a Word from the Lord to encourage, build up and give hope to the family, she continued to seek God for that one special verse. On January 3rd, 2018 it was confirmed to her: Isaiah 61. In her devotional journal it is titled "The Year of the Lord's Favor."

I share this excerpt from her journal with her blessing:

> *Isaiah 61*
>
> *The Spirit of the Lord God is upon me; because the Lord hath anointed me to preach good tidings unto the meek; he hath sent me to bind up the brokenhearted, to proclaim liberty to the captives,*

and the opening of the prison to them that are bound;

To proclaim the acceptable year of the Lord, and the day of vengeance of our God; to comfort all that mourn;

To appoint unto them that mourn in Zion, to give unto them beauty for ashes, the oil of joy for mourning, the garment of praise for the spirit of heaviness; that they might be called trees of righteousness, the planting of the Lord, that he might be glorified.

And they shall build the old wastes, they shall raise up the former desolations, and they shall repair the waste cities, the desolations of many generations.

And strangers shall stand and feed your flocks, and the sons of the alien shall be your plowmen and your vinedressers.

But ye shall be named the Priests of the Lord: men shall call you the Ministers of our God: ye shall eat the riches of the Gentiles, and in their glory shall ye boast yourselves.

For your shame ye shall have double; and for confusion they shall rejoice in their portion: therefore in their land they shall possess the double: everlasting joy shall be unto them.

For I the Lord love judgment, I hate robbery for burnt offering; and I will direct their work in truth, and I will make an everlasting covenant with them.

And their seed shall be known among the Gentiles, and their offspring among the people: all that see them shall acknowledge them, that they are the seed which the Lord hath blessed.

I will greatly rejoice in the Lord, my soul shall be joyful in my God; for he hath clothed me with the garments of salvation, he hath covered me with the robe of righteousness, as a bridegroom decketh himself with ornaments, and as a bride adorneth herself with her jewels.

For as the earth bringeth forth her bud, and as the garden causeth the things that are sown in it to spring forth; so the Lord God will cause righteousness and praise to spring forth before all the nations.

Her entry on Jul 31 is as follows:

"Continuing to the year so far: Lord you have kept your promise of the Lord's favor. I have seen my mother-in-law in a life or death situation in the form of a brain tumor. The operation took half the time during which there was a calling to prayer simultaneously in two completely separate locations (of the hospital). Christy, Dad and their friends upstairs, and I was nudged downstairs to pray at the same time (this was not accomplished on my end due

to kid craziness). During this time the news was shared that you did it again and the tumor was benign. Her recovery was also half the time even with a blood clot.

The best part it all was that this life or death experience is exactly what it took to turn her tears over Anna and turn them to joy. She is still sad over it, but she changed you can see a renewed spirit all over her.

Through all of this, I am moving forward knowing that we will continue to see lives changed in Jesus' Name through Anna's murder and this family's faithfulness. We trust you Lord even when it seems impossible. Nothing is impossible for you!

I also push forward knowing that either here or in eternity we will receive justice for our sister and also help our hearts to love the way you love, because truly how funny would it be if the person who was so mad at our sister that he decided to snatch her away from this earth so he never had to see her again, receives salvation and forgiveness and ends up with her in eternity!

Lord, we are human and with things we are angry and incapable of a love like yours in situations like this. Forgive me, forgive us."

When she shared with me 2018 would be a year of the Lord's Favor, I immediately thought about what it meant to "me." My mind translated into peacefulness, no more sorrow or heartache, a year without any more crises or challenges. A time to embrace our grieving, to be able to absorb and deal with the continuing shock of losing our daughter, and a time to ease into the land of the living and find some balance to our lives. I wanted to go on vacation, to rest and relax and enjoy the simple pleasures of life again. To see color, vibrancy, to feel something besides this sorrow that is buried deep in my soul.

In retrospect, God had another—better—plan for our family. His Favor was with us through our journey into this medical crisis we had faced. We had assurances from His Word, every step of the way. God did show Himself mighty on our behalf.

THE FAVOR OF THE LORD WAS STRONG AND MIGHTY IN 2018!

We have faith to believe, that regardless of circumstances, HE will continue to show us Favor from His strong and mighty Right Hand.

Chapter Twenty-seven: Hold Hands...And Stay Together

In May of 2015 I wrote a thought-provoking devotional entitled, "Hold Hands and Stay Together." I want to share this with you, as you complete the reading of our story. Life is short, fleeting, so whatever challenges you face in your life, whatever disturbances you encounter, whether it is relational, health, or some other crisis, "Hold Hands, and Stay Together." This is the "why" of our family's unity, love and care, the bond that we share. Why we are a team! This was demonstrated and taught to my kids as they grew up.

Stand firm, stand fast in the power of His might! He will uphold you with his right hand of righteousness!

Provoking Thoughts...

I have to write this...the thoughts behind it are compelling me...it won't leave me alone...so here goes. If the shoe fits, wear it or pass it along to someone else who may need to hear this.

"Hold hands and stay together..."

Does this strike you? Commitment, loyalty, support, caring, compassion...hold hands with someone today...show and tell them you love them, care for them, and support them. And then do it for all of the tomorrows you are blessed to have.

Reach across any bridge that is broken in relationships and do your best to mend them; you only have today. And with God's help, it will mend/heal.

As a grandmother of fourteen, I am privileged to be a part of each one's life and adventures, their milestones. Why is this important, you might ask? Grand-parenting is the "reward" of raising your own children or being "adopted" into someone's family.

One of our Sunday school lessons included mentoring, being involved in, and helping those around us, those who will allow that in their life. I am aware of families that are fractured, broken, disassociated with their dear ones. Yes, sometimes there are valid reasons, boundaries we must set for emotional, physical, and spiritual safety.

Sometimes, it is more insecurity and selfishness that causes these hurt feelings and broken relationships.

Without getting detailed—and yes, I am including myself in this challenge—bridge the gap, sacrifice what is necessary, do the right thing and mend broken fences of relationship. When there are young children involved, set petty grievances aside and be there for them. Show them the way of a good life, one dedicated to the Lord, committed to their family, their friends, their church, their community. Show compassion, forgiveness, mercy, long suffering, gentleness, meekness, peacefulness, joy, love. There are ways to be civil without being "chummy," without attitudes and bad behavior. If you KNEW your actions would chart the course of some young child's life, would you change course? If it would make the difference between that young impressionable child being a responsible and fully functioning, self-supporting and loving adult...would you?

I surely hope and pray so.

Hold hands and stay together.

II Corinthians 1:3,4 tells us:

Blessed be God, even the Father of our Lord Jesus Christ, the Father of mercies, and the God of all comfort;

Who comforteth us in all our tribulation, that we may be able to comfort them which are in any trouble, by the comfort wherewith we ourselves are comforted of God.

Our desire is to share our story, and in so doing, be a comfort and help to those who may experience grief through the loss of a loved one or a medical diagnosis that was unexpected. We wish to encourage others in their confusion and helplessness as they face unknown futures.

Traumas of life are some of the hardest burdens to bear. Our prayer is that our story be a comfort, an encouragement to those of you who are dealing with life traumas.

Mercy and Peace to you as you journey this pilgrim road toward Eternal Life!

Epilogue: Thinking Through Various Thoughts

I opted out of attending prayer meeting last night, so I hear this second hand, from my daughter in love, who did go to prayer meeting.

Dr. Stone, our pastor, spoke about Job, how God chose him specifically because God the Father knew he would be faithful and true to Him.

I am humbled and still in shock...I do not feel worthy of God's choice for me, of our family, to be ambassadors of His Grace, Comfort, Compassion, and tender loving care through our grief. I do not understand God's ways, nor His path for our lives.

I do submit to His calling, His Direction, His Gentle sustaining Spirit to bring us aid through so many people, sermons, prayers, especially through His Word.

Blessed be your name, in the land marked with suffering, though there's pain in the offering, blessed be your name!

This song has taken on new meaning, heartfelt and real, a painfully emotional song...I sing it now with tears in my eyes, gushing hole of hurt and pain in my heart, as I embrace this new lifestyle we are living without Daughter.

The pain of losing a child is vastly immense, unexplainable, and incomprehensible, especially in the way we lost Daughter. Pastor mentioned that as well; I am thankful I was not there, as he could speak freely without worrying how it would impact my feelings. We have a kind-hearted, compassionate, and understanding man in the pulpit.

God has seen us through every detail of this nightmare experience. He has stood beside us: Lead us and guided us, given direction and Spoken through His Word things that have taken on new meaning to our souls and spirits.

I have every assurance Father God will continue to do this for us; because of HIS great love and care for us, we will continue to be steadfast in our commitment to love Him and serve Him and to share His wonderful and great love that HE desires for each of us.

Grace and Peace to you as you navigate this journey of Life; May God himself bring Peace to your souls. In Jesus' Name, AMEN

Anna – Remembering

Yours was a heart full of joy and love for the Lord, your children, family
and friends; your lilting voice, melodious and sweet with song,
wafts through our hearts and minds:

We Remember.

Breezes blowing softly through the grass, birds chirping their morning
song, the sun shining in all its radiance: the song of the Whippoorwill
that you so loved: the great outdoors that you thrived in:

We remember.

Wildflowers tucked behind your ear, your graceful pace as you walked
in nature's playground, the peacefulness you loved,
surrounded by nature's bounty:

We remember.

Helping hands extended to offer assistance, Concern for those less
fortunate, Sympathy for those wounded, hurting souls:

We remember.

We remember, we miss, and we mourn. Yet, we rejoice, knowing
there will be a joyous reunion at Heaven's Gate. Embracing with much
Love, and anticipation of joy that awaits...Until we see Heaven's Gate.

We remember....

ANNA LOUISE BROWN
December 31, 1978 - April 30, 2017
(On Anna's 2nd Anniversary of her death)

115

Brevity of Life...A Devotional
August 31, 2018

Life...happens, it is inevitable, it is a beginning, and an end. Usually, we are born with the highest of hopes and dreams, our parents often mesmerized with thoughts of perfection and starry eyes in their little twinkle-eyed bundle of joy.

Our existence has a heartbeat of its own, a path and direction yet unknown. Many twists and turns, adventures with joy and sorrow, excitement and thrill await us as we develop into an adult, our very own personhood.

Then...tragedy strikes. A car accident, a diagnosis of incurable disease, a crisis of unimaginable magnitude; a loved one changes course and departs for a different life than what we envisioned.

How in the world does one cope? Our minds are overwhelmed with thoughts of inadequacy, failure, the "what if's" swirling around in our troubled hearts and souls.

Is there hope? Is there direction, a sense of peace or acceptance in the trouble one faces?

Faith in God should be a strong component of one's existence; it takes faith to believe in the sanctity and value of life. Faith is necessary to embrace the storms that will present themselves over the course of our time here on earth. Faith based on our loving and omnipotent Heavenly Father will never fail us. It is a shelter in the storms of life, a protector during times of testing, a supporter that lifts us up and breathes life, hope, healing, love and endurance into our wearied souls and hearts.

How does one know this with certainty, you might ask? The infallible Word spoken by God himself has been preserved throughout the ages, speaks truth, life, love and forgiveness to us if we will seek, knock, find. Our hearts will be stilled, our souls bathed in the balm of His tender loving care and protection.

That the trial of your faith (the difficulties you face ...) being much more precious than of gold that perisheth, though it be tried with fire, might be found unto praise and honour and glory at the appearing of Jesus Christ... (I Peter 1:7).

But seek ye first the kingdom of God, and His righteousness, and all these things shall be added unto you (Matt 6:33a).

My brethren, count it all joy when ye fall into divers temptations; knowing this, that the trying of your faith worketh patience. But let patience have her perfect work, that ye may be perfect and entire, wanting nothing (James 1:2, 3).

Embrace Him, His Word, His Hope, and His Love. It makes the journey worthwhile...eternally.

The Whippoorwill

All is quiet All is still

Waiting for the trill

Of a whippoorwill.

Oh magnificent, oh praise be

His thrilling, trilling

Song

Just sung for me!

All is quiet all is still;

I hear the song of the whippoorwill.

Moon rising high in the night sky;

All I can do is...sigh...

Or

Cry.

"Deep great trials
bring with them
deep grace
from God….

All of which
enlarges our soul's
capacity
for
Jesus."

(Taken from video broadcast on Joni Eareckson Tada's 52nd diving accident anniversary, July 30, 2019, used with permission.)

Birthing a Book

While home recuperating from brain surgery, I was often awake because of the steroids I was prescribed. This was a challenge for me to occupy myself while the rest of the house was sleeping.

In one of the early morning hours about 2 am, I had a sudden brainstorm—no pun intended! I had known I would write a book at some point in my life and had been considering it seriously in the last traumatic year. I was aware of the three-month recovery period I would have, so began planning to use that time wisely. I kept a pen and notebook beside me, so I grabbed it and began writing. First, I wrote chapter titles without hesitation: Just jotted them down so I could remember contents and story line for each one. They came to me, rapid fire, as if Someone was directing my thoughts! Initially, there were twenty-four topics to cover, or chapters. That would be revised as the book came to life. Then, the title was born out of the contents of the book. The original title has been revised to a different one, and the original one became part of the current sub-title. God is good in His direction and leading.

It has been a bittersweet experience writing this journey of ours. Daughter would be proud, as she knew I wanted to write. As a writer herself, she understood the need to put pen and paper together, and let words bloom into thoughts and fragrant petals on the pages of journals.

Our saga continues, our life plods along; sometimes peacefully, sometimes with sorrowful willpower propelling us to continue. We continue in Faith, because the One who has sustained us thus far is the Keeper of our Souls, the Faithful One who carries us when we don't have the fortitude to function.

God is Faithful.

Grief never ends...
but it changes.
It's a passage,
not a place to stay.
Grief is not a sign
of weakness,
nor a lack of faith...
It is the price of
Love.
~Author Unknown

121

About the author:

Sue Lamb Brown grew up in a rural area of Northwest Florida. As a farmer's daughter she experienced a full and active life and had many adventures participating on a working farm.

After attending Troy State University, she married her high school sweetheart. They settled in the community she grew up in and began their life together, merging their work and family into the dynamics of the area. While primarily a stay at home mom of five children, Sue, along with her husband, was involved in Inner City Ministry for several years. She has served as a caregiver for the elderly as well as operating several small startup businesses. Upon retirement, the author has focused on ministry to her family, especially enjoying her fourteen grandchildren.

She has enjoyed many pioneering type hobbies, such as sewing, preservation of foods, cooking for her large family, gardening, and managing a small blueberry pick and pay operation.

It is not unusual to find her in her favorite swing with a glass of sweet iced tea and a good book.

About the book:

In her debut autobiography, Sue Lamb Brown has written a concise and compelling narrative of her life. Focusing on two main crises that her family experienced, she has expressed with heartfelt emotion the highs and lows of these events and how they have impacted her family, friends, and community.

The resolve and determination to rise from the ashes of grief and heartache to hope and joy, motivated her family to keep going toward healing and wholeness. Sustained by her faith, the author shares a riveting and encouraging, hope-filled healing message with her audience. She desires to be a blessing and help to all those who read her story and may travel a similar journey of their own.

Made in the USA
Coppell, TX
27 November 2019